BOULDER

The inside story of an extraordinary 2015 season

TOM SMITH
(with Ken Grime)

Max Books

© Tom Smith 2016

First published in the UK in 2016 by Max Books

The right of Tom Smith to be identified as the Author of this work has been asserted by them in accordance with the Copyright, Designs and Patents Act 1988

A CIP catalogue record for this title is available from the British Library

ISBN: 978-0-9934872-1-7

Typeset and Design by Andrew Searle

Photography: David Griffin, Simon Pendrigh, Barry Mitchell

Printed and bound by CPI Ltd

MAX BOOKS
Epworth House
34 Wellington Road
Nantwich Cheshire CW5 7BX
Tel: 01270 625278
Email: maxcricket@btinternet.com
www.max-books.co.uk

Contents

Foreword by Holly Smith   5

Diary

April: A perfect start, and then...   13

May: Second eleven comeback   29

June: Rehab and recovery   63

July: The worst of days, the best day   99

August: Winning and grinning   135

September: Pilates and promotion   171

Postscript: On the road to recovery   193

Foreword

by Holly Smith

THERE AREN'T many people in the world who can say they are living their dream. For Tom though, that is 100% the case. Cricket isn't just a job to him, it's his childhood dream, his passion and I can't think of anyone else who deserves it more.

I've known Tom since I was eight years old and I remember it being a rare occasion seeing him without his whites on and cricket bag in tow. Cricket was always the plan for him and nothing else seemed to matter.

I know I'm biased, but I feel my perception of Tom is quite fair and shared with most who know him. Tom is a modest man and very rarely performs any kind of selfish act. He is solely in it just for the love of the game and doesn't particularly like any limelight that comes with the territory. He is very highly thought of amongst friends and colleagues. You absolutely know he would do anything for anyone if he could. He is a fantastic husband (when he listens!) and I know he will be a fantastic father to our little spud cooking away as I write. With this in mind, it makes this all the more hard to think back to his experience over the last year or so. A tough one to say the least.

2014 was by far the most memorable year for him, and us. Tom had the best season of his career, receiving an England Lions call-up, awarded Lancashire Player of the Year, and getting to the NatWest T20 final and so on. Personally though, he was on fire!! I was a very proud wife to be and I remember it so well having been asked a few times what I had been feeding him that season. I wish I could take the blame for it but I felt this had been brewing for a while now. Constant setbacks with injuries in previous seasons had just fuelled his fire even more!

However, with the highs, also came the lows and he finished the season with a back spasm which ruled him out of the last game. Not bad going though considering his achievements. He was still a happy chappy and we looked forward to the coming months in the run up to our wedding in December. A perfect end to the year! However, we didn't know then that the back spasm was the start of a major setback in his career and the next year was going to be very challenging for him.

When we returned from our honeymoon in January 2015 Tom found out he had been given the honour of becoming club captain. A speechless Tom rang me at work and it took a while for him to spit out what he was trying to say through the ear to ear grin on his face. For all who know Tom and who had played a part in his life or career, this was a very proud moment to witness. A young lad from Withnell Fold who once dreamed of playing for his county, now that dream was reality and he had earned something much greater which he had never even thought possible!

The run-up to the 2015 season was an exciting one with Tom taking to his new role like a duck to water. He was eager to kick start the season with a bang. And he did just that...

During his first game as captain, Tom developed another back spasm and after being ruled out for a couple of months, his frustrations began to appear as I'm sure they would with anyone. However, he managed to recover and set off to play in a second team game in hope he could pick up where he left off.... I was very nervous for him; lord knows how Tom was feeling.

I didn't realise at first just how serious these spasms were, and that they were an indication that something wasn't right and could pose a threat to Tom's career. When I received a phone call at work halfway through the game, I knew it wasn't good news. He never rings me during a game and I just knew what he was going to tell me. I stared at my phone for a few seconds before I answered it with my stomach churning. Sure enough it was another spasm and Tom was on his way to the hospital to get a scan on his back. I will never forget the sound of his voice on the phone. He was close to tears; very quiet and subdued.

It is never nice to see a loved one upset, angry or worried and naturally you want to protect them and say everything will be okay. When we finally got the nod from Tom's physio and the specialist that he was to have surgery it took all of my strength not to cry in front of him. I'm not sure he knows this actually, I think that he thinks I was just being a hard-faced cow at the time! I wasn't too worried about the surgery, I knew that he was in good hands and the recovery rate for this surgery was high and in his favour. I had gone online and googled the surgery a lot and found out that Tiger Woods and Andy Murray had very similar back ops. That put my mind at rest a little. For me, it was more about the sheer frustration and mental exhaustion I knew this would cause Tom. He had proven his talent that year, he had achieved so much and just when he had it all in the grasp of his hands, this happened. He didn't deserve it and it took a while for us both to get our heads around. It all happened very quickly though and in a space of a week he was in and out of hospital having had the op.

There were some very tough times throughout his recovery, for us both, and it's hard to pin-point any moments exactly where it was particularly low. Tom wasn't shy of an injury throughout his career. There had always been the odd tweak or niggle, but this was different. He was extremely worried about his future in the game too, and it was very scary to watch especially when there is nothing you can do to help.

Tom was pretty much bed bound for a good few weeks after surgery and there is only so much reading and watching TV one can do. He can never sit still at the best of times and having to rely on his wife help him out of bed and walk him to the bathroom, to shower and feed him, he hated every minute!! I could see his mind wander off into dark places at times. He would start to lose faith and become very negative. His good friend Kyle Hogg had to retire the previous year due to a back condition and I knew that was playing on his mind. He would start to worry about life after cricket, which would in time turn into money worries etc. Cricket is his life, what would he do? I let him vent his worries at first, and just listened as I knew he just needed an ear, but I'm more of a tough love kind of person and there was only so much doom and gloom I would allow. To him though it seemed like he wasn't making any progress fast enough but to myself and everyone else around him, we could see he was.

At a point where it was all becoming very consuming, an exciting turn of events proved life has an amazing way of telling you everything will be okay. We found out a month or so after his surgery that we were to become parents in March 2016. You could see a change in Tom straight away after this. He became focused, determined and the hardworking Tom reappeared. He would soon have another person who would rely on him and this was more than enough for him to pledge that he would get fit again, he would go back to doing what he loves and he wasn't going to let another injury stop him.

Tom started to make a diary from the early stages of recovery and constantly took notes about his day to day routine, frustrations, Lancs performances and ways he could try to help out. He was in constant contact with Ashley Giles, Steven Croft and Paul

Horton wanting to be kept involved. He would text the lads words of encouragement and congratulations. He would always listen to them play on Radio Lancashire, watch on TV and follow scores. At first, it was something for him to do, something to distract him from not actually playing himself. The thought of going back to being captain was something that pushed him even harder. From my point of view it almost seemed like torture and broke my heart to see him desperately try and keep hold of that.

When the season had drawn to a close and Tom watched with pride as the lads won their T20 victory, his focus now had to be solely on his recovery as he could see Steven Croft was doing an amazing job at captaining the side. The thought of not being ready for the 2016 season still loomed over him. He knew that he must now focus this winter on his progression and training. This in time led to Tom stepping down as captain, a decision he did not take lightly. It was a sad time for him and a decision that he has made, he says, from a selfish point of view, albeit he did it for his personal development and to focus on himself and for no other reason. However, I feel differently about this. I think it's also from a selfless point of view. He knew the team had adapted well to Steven as captain and didn't want to interfere with that. He knew the club needed consistency with their captain and Tom wasn't at a point where he could offer this. There was also the question of how long it would take him to 'fully' recover. Tom deliberated hard on this and even asked several people's opinions. He finally came to the decision that it was best for himself and the club to step down. He was over the moon to have been asked and didn't want to come across as being ungrateful for having been offered the opportunity, but he felt right about his decision and he still does to this day. More so he's happy that the captaincy was awarded to Steven Croft. Steven is a good friend to Tom and a fantastic teammate and he couldn't think of anyone better to take over. He then spent the rest of the winter concentrating on himself and it has paid off one hundred percent!

This brings us to the present and I can't quite believe how much Tom has come on since his spinal surgery in July last year. He is a completely different person both mentally and physically. He is back to training full time with his teammates, batting and bowling and very much looking forward to the pre-season tour in Dubai and the prospect of making a comeback this year. It just shows what a positive spin on things and a constant support network can do for someone.

Tom finally saw the light at the end of the tunnel. Sometimes this light would appear to be an oncoming train in his eyes but he would always find a way to get past negative thoughts. Even if it was a result of an ear-bashing from me telling him to snap out of it! There were many times when we had to remind ourselves how lucky we were and that things could only get better, but, as testing as it was, here we are today, approaching the 2016 season with a fantastic chance of a full recovery. We will surely be glad to see the back of this experience… no pun intended. It definitely calls for the saying 'what doesn't kill you only makes you stronger'.

I would like to take this opportunity to thank a number of people in our lives for getting Tom to where he is now. Dave Roberts and his wife Kim and Sam Byrne and the rest of the physio and strength and conditioning team at Lancashire CCC. You have played a huge role in his recovery and he wouldn't be where he is today without any of you.

To Ashley Giles and all of Tom's teammates, including Paul Horton, Ashwell Prince and Kyle Hogg. You all kept Tom upbeat and focused and made it very easy for him to talk to you and make important decisions along the way. Thank you!

To our family and friends, including all the players' partners and families. You have all been very supportive from day one and kept me sane in the process. You have been a huge support network for Tom and I and we couldn't have gotten through it without you.

To all the people who sent Tom positive and kind messages of support throughout his recovery. It was always nice to hear and read on a particularly tough day.

And lastly to my husband... No matter how hard it was, how tough you found it, you always seemed to bounce back. You have been my rock throughout pregnancy, even though you had so much on your mind. I am so very proud of you and you are true inspiration to us all. I know you will continue to amaze me for years to come. Bump and I love you lots. Keep going - you're almost there!

Holly, February 2016

APRIL

A perfect start, and then…

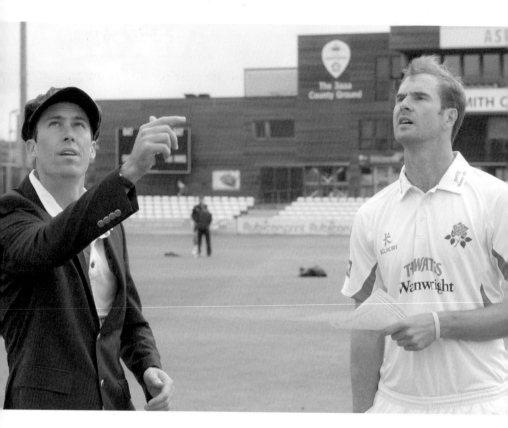

Opening Day: out in the middle for the toss at Derby

19th April

THE SEASON is finally here, and we are starting our campaign with a Championship game at Derby.

Everyone was disappointed last year with relegation but the feeling amongst the camp is a confidence that we will put it right. Promotion is a key target for us but, as we have done in the past, the intention to be competitive on all fronts is a priority.

I was extra early turning up this morning, and with all the excitement I didn't get a great deal of sleep last night. All our preparations have been good and everyone now just wants to get up and running.

Giving my first team talk that morning I was nervous, yet excited, all of a sudden. Of all the advice given to me before this moment two things stuck out: 'Only speak when you need to' and 'less is more'.

After some deliberation, and a check on the wicket, the final eleven was chosen - and then it hit me. Now I am captain I would have to inform those not playing. This is part of the role and when accepting the job I knew there would be times where tough decisions had to be made.

I will never forget walking out to toss up that first time. All my family were there to see it and my brother had flown over especially from Germany to be there. I lost the toss, and we got stuck in which wasn't the greatest start!

The wicket was green and slightly damp - bowler friendly you could say. That showed when we were 5-2, and then 55-4 when I went in.

Alviro (Petersen) is new to the club but having seen him bat before, and being on the wrong end of an innings of 150 then, we knew all about his talent and class. Today that showed. I had the best seat in the house at the other end to see his century. I found batting tough, but knew I just had to battle to get some runs. Anything to help get us near a total of 250 - which would be a great score.

It was amazing to have my family down to be with me today to experience it all as well. A traditional curry family meal took place in the evening, although an early night is needed as tomorrow is going to be a big day.

20th April

WE MANAGED to get to 293, which was massive. We have good depth in our order with Peter Siddle (Sids) batting at no.8. In the context of the game this could be crucial as we move forward.

I knew at the start our attack would be handy on this wicket. Sids our overseas player certainly showed his class in his first spell. Maybe nine overs was one to many but he could have had nine wickets! Slater was first to go with a little nick to Al (Davies) then he produced a peach to get rid of Guptill. I caught the edge high and right, we got on a bit of a role and quickly had them in trouble at 26-3. Sids aside, me, Bails (Tom Bailey) and Jarv (Kyle Jarvis) didn't bowl that well.

Durston chanced his arm a bit and it came off. He got a run-a-ball 85 which got them up to 274-a lot more than we were hoping for.

To their credit Derbyshire came out and bowled well. They bowled a fuller length with Footitt bowling a fast and ferocious spell. We finished on 36-3 in our second innings, which was not ideal, and it makes the first hour tomorrow vital.

21st April

THE TEAM talk was simple this morning; we knew what we had to do. The lads were motivated. Ashwell Prince has a saying, one he often uses: 'you can score a hundred to win a game or save a game'. He showed all his experience and class today and his partnership with Crofty changed the game.

Alviro and myself fell early. I played a poor shot pushing in front of me. I did feel a little bit of extra pressure as captain to get a score and went away from what I do well. Let the bowler bowl to me!!

But I desperately wanted a win in my first game as captain; I've never wanted it more.

We got to 245-9, a lead of 264, which was something to bowl at and we felt confident at that point. However a last wicket stand is always good. It flattens the opposition just when they think they are done. If you score 20-30 you would be happy with that. One hundred runs later, and after some of the best ball striking from Alex, we had a lead of 364. This was massive. The mental aspect of chasing a score like that after thinking you might only need 270-280 is huge.

It all worked in our favour today. The cheeky half hour that was left meant Derbyshire had to bat out the day. Never nice for opening batsman! Getting two out tonight was vital to how tomorrow was going to be shaped. I had dinner with the lads in the hotel, just chatting about cricket and tactics for the following day. Going to bed I felt confident but there is lots of work still to be done.

22nd April

FAIR TO say I didn't get a lot of sleep last night! Thoughts of how the day could pan out kept running through my head. We need eight wickets with 336 runs left in the bank.

I knew a couple of quick ones would seal it for us, but the early breakthrough didn't come until Jarv was introduced into the attack. Once he got Guptill there was no stopping him. He ran in hard and bowled with good pace and aggression. It took us just 41 overs to bowl them out and Jarv finished with 5-13 off 9 overs. It was an amazing spell.

We had to work hard for this win, and it really was a team effort. Somewhere along the line everyone contributed.

My back gave me some trouble today which wasn't great. I was stiff all down my left side. Fingers crossed, it's just a reaction to playing again. I managed to get through my spell though, and bowled a lot better than the first dig which was pleasing.

It has been an amazing few days. I've learnt a lot about myself as a captain, and there are a lot of good cricket minds in our team which is handy. I will need their help along the way.

LV=County Championship Division Two
Game 1 at Derby, 19-22 April

Lancashire 293 (Petersen 115) & 345
(Prince 97, Davies 89, Croft 70, Taylor 6-61)
Derbyshire 274 (Durston 85, Godleman 76,
Kerrigan 3-21) & 114 (Jarvis 5-13, Bailey 3-38)

Lancashire won by 250 runs

A century on his Lancashire debut by Alviro Peterson, 97 by Ashwell Prince, and a decisive five-wicket blast from Kyle Jarvis helped the Red Rose start their 2015 County Championship campaign in fine style. Led by new skipper Tom Smith, Lancashire won by the comfortable margin of 250 runs but the game was evenly poised until well into the third day.

Peterson's 115, the seventh century by a Lancashire player on debut, was instrumental in the visitors' first innings total of 293 but Derbyshire hit back well with 274 largely thanks to Wes Durston's aggressive 85.

Lancashire posted a healthy total of 345, underpinned by 97 for Prince, second time around before the hosts closed the third day on 27-2. Steven Croft's 70 and an entertaining best innings of 89 from Alex Davies really stamped Lancashire's authority on the match, with the latter sharing in a record tenth-wicket stand of 100 with Jarvis, who made an invaluable 17 not out.

Jarvis then bowled Lancashire to victory with a memorable morning five-wicket burst on day four, returned his best figures in a Red Rose shirt of 5-13 as Derby, chasing 365, slipped from 77-3 to 105-8, with the 26-year-old taking all five wickets inside his first seven overs.

Derbyshire's tail end could not extend the match beyond lunch and they were bowled out for 114 inside 42 overs.

23rd April

WOKE UP today feeling very sore and stiff. This is normally the case after a four-day game although this felt different. My back felt really sore on the left side, it had pretty much gone into spasm. I've suffered these before and knew that it meant a minimum week out.

Going in to see Sam (Byrne, LCCC Physiotherapist) I could already predict what he was going to say.

The game against Kent starts on Sunday which is only a couple of days away. I was desperate to play, after starting with a win - it was a chance to build some real momentum.

I tried telling him I would be fine, but we both knew deep down that I would be missing the game. This was the sensible option and all my energy would now be going into getting right for the next game.

24th April

UNFORTUNATELY THERE aren't many ways to cure a back spasm. A period of rest and a course of ibuprofen is the general regime.

Today has mostly been spent lying down watching films with the odd trip to the kitchen thrown in-not what I was expecting to be doing two weeks into my tenure as captain! Spasms can happen at any time and really are crippling. You soon learn how much you use your back in day-to-day activities and how we take it for granted.

As boring as the next few days are going to be it's vital to my recovery and getting fit for the Northants game that starts a week on Sunday.

25th April

I'M SLOWLY seeing signs of improvement. Today my movements are becoming easier and feeling a lot more natural. I was allowed a ten minute walk to try and get the muscles in my lower back moving, thus relieving the spasm.

I'm feeling pretty gutted that I won't be playing tomorrow. Last season I managed to stay fit for the majority of the season, which certainly helped my performances. Hopefully this is just a blip for this season. A lot of doing nothing was prescribed again, but I did get to spend a Saturday with my new wife Holly which can be a rare thing in the cricket season, so I guess it wasn't all bad!

26th April

GAME DAY for the boys. Driving into the ground, ideas were going through my mind of how Kent may play and how we could go about getting win number two for the season. Kent are a strong side with some high class players; they are a team you can't underestimate.

I was gutted not to be playing but this gave us the chance to hand Jordan Clark his first-class debut. It's great seeing players faces when they find out their dreams have come true. I was chuffed to bits for Clarky. He had shown massive improvement in the winter and certainly warranted his selection.

The wicket looked a belter, a typical Old Trafford pitch. Unlike me, Crofty won the toss and with no hesitation batted. It was frustrating not to play but it gave me chance to see the game from a different perspective and take note of different things.

Ashwell made a brilliant century. He couldn't have played any better; the way he constructed his innings was a pleasure to watch. For me it was a short walk at lunch and tea to try and work this spasm out of my back. This didn't help my frustration but I knew I was heading in the right direction. What did cheer me up was coming back to a homemade Sunday roast. A great way to end the day.

27th April

MOVED REALLY well this morning. My back felt great, and the rest seems to have done the trick. I couldn't wait to get a bat back in my hands and go into the nets. After a chat Sam and I decided to leave it for a day. There was no need to rush and jump straight back in just yet-letting my back completely settle was the main focus. Other than walking and some light lumbar exercises nothing else could be achieved today. I am getting a lot closer to playing again though.

28th April

WE DID play some outstanding cricket today. If someone offered you 99 every time you went out bat I'm sure every batter would take it. Alex (Davies) played a mature, sensible innings following on from the one last week against Derby. My heart sank when on 99 he nicked one to second slip and what would have been his maiden hundred fell just out of reach. It was a great knock and if he continues to play as he is, I'm sure he will score plenty of centuries.

The bowlers backed up last week with another outstanding display on a pitch that couldn't be more different. The discipline they showed was terrific because they had to graft for every wicket. It was what you would call 'proper cricket'.

Not getting in the nets today was disappointing though. It makes tomorrow seem that bit more exciting. I just want to play.

29th April

CAME TO the ground itching to get started. While the boys were getting ready for an important final day, I was busy doing some simple underarm drills with Sam before having a net. Getting padded up, it was like all my Christmases had come at once.

After hitting a few balls I felt my back aching again but I ploughed through thinking all would be okay. It wasn't. The aching got worse to the point where I could feel a spasm coming on. I went to see Sam who immediately got me into a resting position.

I knew things weren't great. After a chat with Sam and 'Rooster' (Dave Roberts, LCCC Head Physiotherapist) it was decided that I would go for another scan. MRI machines are certainly not much fun to be in. Over the years I've got used to them, but it generally means something is up when you're in one!

LV= County Championship Division Two
Game 2 at Emirates Old Trafford, 26-29 April

Lancashire 444 (Prince 106, Davies 99, Horton 71, Claydon 4-103) & 107-1 (Horton 67*)
Kent 252 (Northeast 55, Jarvis 4-50) & following-on 295 (Denly 60, Jarvis 4-67, Siddle 3-36)

Lancashire won by 9 wickets

Lancashire continued their good start to the season with a thrilling nine-wicket victory over Kent, clinched with just 14 balls to spare on a dramatic final afternoon at Old Trafford.

Ashwell Prince struck 106-his third consecutive century for the Red Rose against Kent-after Steven Croft, deputising for the injured Tom Smith, won the toss while Alex Davies agonisingly fell one run short of a maiden first-class 'ton' in Lancashire's total of 444.

Kyle Jarvis, with three wickets in 22 balls and on his way to figures of 4-50, put the skids under Kent's reply and the visitors could only muster 252 as the Red Rose attack shared the rest of the wickets.

Following-on, it looked like a combination of the weather and some strong resistance by the Kent batsman on the final day might deny the Red Rose, but once the visitors were bowled out for 295 mid-way through the evening session, Lancashire were not to be denied. Jarvis again did the damage with 4-67 and Aussie quick Peter Siddle took 3-36 to leave a winning target of 104 in 21 overs.

Paul Horton and Luis Reece started in positive fashion, taking 26 from the first five overs, to enter the final hour requiring 78 to clinch victory from the remaining 16 overs.

Reece fell for 21 off just 16 balls but Horton took the lead with an outstanding innings of 67 not out from 62 balls, including seven fours and one huge six, to steer Lancashire home, the only major concern arriving when the umpires conferred over the light with 24 runs needed and six overs left.

30th April

SWEATING ON my results today. Deep down I know it's not going to be great news and I feel another extended time sat on the side-lines is inevitable. It's never nice being injured-especially when it means being out for a long time! Fingers crossed it's not as bad as I think.

MAY

Second eleven comeback

A return to action with the Seconds

1st May

GOT THE results of my scan back and the result I feared was correct. A bulging disc in my back was aggravating the spinal nerve causing the spasms in my back. I knew this was going to be a long layoff but not one you can't return from. Sam has booked me in to see the specialist who may be able to provide some route to recovery. At least the West Indies v England series in the Caribbean is on the TV which will hopefully give me something to watch.

A month of the season has flown by already and we've had a great start to the campaign with two wins in the opening two games. Early season momentum is crucial in getting yourself and the team moving - you can take it into the other competitions as the season moves on. It also creates a positive mood in the camp.

The lads are getting ready for the Northampton game. Northants are a strong team who were relegated with us last year, so I'm sure they will be looking to put on a good show and bounce back just as we are hoping to.

2nd May

GREAT TO see Alastair Cook go to a century in the Test Match out in Barbados. He's been getting a bit of stick recently which is certainly not called for. He's going to go down as one of England's best ever players. I'm sure he will smash all of the batting records. I'm really looking forward to the Ashes but everyone seems to be writing us off so quickly. Yet in English conditions there is no one better than Jimmy Anderson. I think it will be closer than most think.

3rd May

WELL THE Test Match certainly moved forward quickly! I don't think anyone expected West Indies to win inside three days. Credit has to be given to the Windies who have some world-class performers and in their own backyard are extremely effective. It's a blow to the England team although I'm still confident that this summer they will surprise a lot of people. We have some box-office players who can turn a game on its head in a session. We need the media to stay behind them and keep backing them.

It looked like a good toss to win at Northants. With the recent poor weather the pitch will have most in it this morning. Looking at the scores though it seems pretty flat, but by all account the weather isn't exactly summerish! With bad weather knocking about a high-scoring draw would be just as good as a win. It's frustrating not being able to go the game and watch. The coverage on BBC local radio is fantastic and Scott Read does a great job on commentary. Not being able to play is really starting to get to me now. I'm looking forward to seeing the specialist but underneath I'm a little scared as to what he will say.

May the 4th be with you! (sorry)

MY BACK is very sore this morning. The spasm has caused a shift in my back with my hips and shoulder about four inches out of line. Simple tasks are now epic feats of movement at the moment.

Mentally it's tough because, as a player, you just want to play. Any sportsperson will tell you being on the side-lines is the hardest thing in the world. You have to keep a positive mind-set and look to the future. Easier said than done!

The Northants game looks like it's going to be a draw. Ashwell seems to be in the form of his life! He could have scored three hundreds in three games after coming so close at Derby. We needed someone to get a score for us and he stood up. Despite my concerns over the weather, from speaking to a couple of the lads, it seems the pitch is batter-friendly. If we go big and go past them then who knows, we could potentially force a result on the last day. Someone will have to go big though.

5th May

WE HAVE a chance! Even though a delayed start meant a lot of the day had been lost we managed to get in front of Northants. Our lower order all love their batting and pride themselves on scoring runs. 'Sids' has scored a few Test fifties so it was no surprise to see him come close to a century. He was ably supported by Tom Bailey who is no mug with the bat. Getting a lead was massive. With Northants two wickets down overnight and still trailing, it puts so much pressure on them in the morning session. Pressure does funny things. Even on the flattest of pitch batting line-ups can crumble. It's going to be a big day tomorrow so let's hope the rain keeps off!

6th May

THE FORECAST doesn't look too crash hot for today's play. The game is delicately poised. If we have a good session this morning then a win is certainly there to be taken. The fact we had to play without bails today says a lot about conditions. Listening intently via the radio it sounded like a hurricane was descending on Wantage Road!

I'm booked into see the specialist tomorrow. I hope its good news! My symptoms seem to be getting better so maybe it won't be as long out as I think. However I feel if I rush this though it could end up a lot worse. It's not long until the T20 starts now and I would love to be fit for that. We are always well supported and it's a strong competition for us. We challenge every year in T20 and came so close last year. Hopefully this year we will go one better.

LV= County Championship Division Two
Game 3 at Northampton, 3-6 May

Northants 385 (Crook 91, Clark 4-101, Jarvis 3-79)
& 391-5 (Keogh 100, Peters 81)
Lancashire 436 (Prince 153, Siddle 89)

Match Drawn

After rain delayed the start until 2.30pm, Northants progressed to 120-1 before closing on 197-6, with two wickets each for Peter Siddle, Jordan Clark and Kyle Jarvis who struck twice in two balls in the last full over of the day. Steven Crook hit an entertaining 91 off 89 balls at the start of day two to help the hosts total a useful looking 385.

Ashwell Prince continued his sparkling start to the new season with another hundred, sharing 112-run partnership with Paul Horton (49) and reaching a memorable 153 on the third day following further rain delays. Siddle made a domestic best 89, adding 100 for the 7th wicket with Prince, and Tom Bailey posted a career-best 34 in Lancashire's 436.

Northants closed on 32-2 but a final day century from Rob Keogh, 81 from Stephen Peters and Crook's 102 not out ensure the draw.

7th May

I WOKE up this morning feeling very apprehensive about my consultation with the specialist. The area of the injury makes it bit more unsettling for me, especially after what happened to Hoggy (Kyle Hogg) who had to retire due to a serious back injury last year.

I met Sam at the office who seemed quite relaxed about the whole thing which helped to put me at ease. Mr Leggate is one of the best in his field; he's the Senior Neurosurgeon at the Greater Manchester Neurosciences Centre. He settled me down in his office and performed some basic tests which he seemed happy with. He then took a look at my scan, explaining in the detail where the bulge was and how it was affecting me. He did mention in all of this that bowling may be a doubt in the future. This took me back at first. I must admit I didn't expect to hear that. He recommended an epidural jab to the enflamed area, as my symptoms were easing and my range of movement increasing. This seemed like a good outcome-well better than surgery anyway! The thought of getting needles shoved in my spine didn't sound too great though. He's managed to fit me in for tomorrow which is handy. Hopefully after this I can put this episode behind me, crack on with my rehab and get back on the field.

8th May

EPIDURAL DAY! I didn't really know what to expect to be honest. Arriving at the hospital I was taken through to the day patients' area and given the funky hospital gowns that you have to wear. Somehow I managed to put it on the wrong way! Sam came with me to make sure everything went according to plan. I was a little nervous going down to theatre, but before I knew it I was back upstairs eating a chicken sandwich. It was over in a flash. I could feel the needle going in but nothing after that due to the anaesthetic in my system. The nurse watched over me for an hour to make sure I had no ill effects from the jab, and then I was free to go. Paul Horton came to pick me up as driving would have been difficult. Strict orders had been given that I had to do nothing for a few days, letting the jab take full effect. I'm hoping that this epidural does the job. I can't wait to get back out there and play some cricket.

Arriving back home, I put the England game on-they were due to take on Ireland in a 50 over game-but looks like the weather is going to win. There is a lot of talk about Peter Moores losing the England job. I hope it's not the case because he's a fantastic coach. I think himself and the team need time to really grow together as a group.

9th May

UNFORTUNATELY IT looks like Moorsey is going to go. The speculation and leaking of information seems to be pointing to only one thing. If that's the case, he should feel really hard done by. The process seems to have been tough on Pete. In my opinion he should have been given more time.

Meanwhile the jab from yesterday seems to be doing its trick. The inflammation in my back seems to be settling gradually. Gloucestershire are the visitors to Old Trafford this week. They have a good mix of junior and senior pros in the team and are not to be taken lightly.

10th May

UP AND about a little bit today, but not able to get into the ground until tomorrow. A light stroll around the block was the rehab for today to get myself moving again. I did stop for a coffee along the way and watched the world go by. I do enjoy some time to myself to reflect on the game and how things are going. It's a chance to really focus on your game and asses what you think is working or may not be. This side of the game I find fascinating, and with the help of the club's psychologist my game has improved.

Gloucester seem to have had a good day, finishing the day on 322-7. Looks like it could be another tough game for the bowlers on a true Old Trafford pitch. It's Peter Siddle's last game for us before he flies off to join Australia in the West Indies. We are all chuffed to bits for him having been selected in the Ashes squad as well. We will miss him greatly as the impact he has made with bat and ball so far has been amazing. Let's hope he signs off in style.

11th May

I WAS excited to get to the ground today, although it was only to do laps of the outfield at lunch and tea. Being back in the changing room is a great feeling. There is no better place and nowhere quite like it.

We needed to knock Gloucs' over early this morning and try to go past them with the bat. All out for 388 was perfect and we would have taken that at the start of the day. Paul Horton then showed all of his class and character to bat out the rest of the day to finish 134 not out. It was proper openers' knock; seeing off the new ball then pressing on and taking control. He formed a valuable partnership with Ashwell for the 3rd wicket after losing two quick ones. Princey fell for 57 just as he looked set for another big one. With other mini partnerships forming we pushed on to 276-6 overnight. Tomorrow is going to be an important day. If we can draw level with them the next two days will provide some entertaining cricket.

Sam seems happy with my progress; I seem to have responded really well to the jab, and may even try some running tomorrow. Rock and roll!

12th May

DRIVING INTO the ground today I was picturing my return to cricket in my head, and how it would feel to bat and bowl again. I kept mentally rehearsing playing my strong shots over and over, remembering how they felt and what it was like to play. I was itching to have a go.

The game is in a delicate state today. A good session for them and we are behind the eight-ball. Fortunately 'Horts' battled on to make 168, ably supported once again by 'Sids' down the order. We fell 24 short of them-it's never nice to concede a first innings lead-but we showed fighting qualities throughout the innings. A good session now for us certainly puts us back on top, and some early breakthroughs would put massive pressure on their middle order. Unfortunately it didn't come; the pitch still looked good for batting and that showed. The early wicket of Dent gave us some encouragement but their overseas player Peter Handscomb ushered them to 206-3 overnight. I played with Pete while I was at St Kilda during the 2008/09 winter in Melbourne. He was only young then, but there was a lot of talk about him being a potential international for Australia. Today he showed how good a player he is.

13th May

THE FINAL day has arrived, and with all three results still possible the prospect of an exciting run chase for us is definitely on the cards. We like to play positive cricket and certainly will have a go at chasing down a target. If we can knock a couple over upfront they could fall in a heap, making our job a lot easier.

Handscomb and Marshall managed to form a good partnership, the latter falling just short of his 100 but it put their team in a commanding position. Bowling them out was a great effort, and 'Sids' signed off with a four-wicket haul showing us all his skills with the ball. He will be missed.

Gloucs' lead was just over 300 with around 70 overs remaining and we really fancied our chances of chasing it down. The pitch was still playing well and we have a strong batting order. Unfortunately we didn't get off to a great start, losing early wickets to some good bowling with the new ball. From being 22-4 Alex and Alviro formed a great partnership to get us back into the game. Then just on the stroke of tea we lost Alex, which shifted the momentum back to them. We were still in a good position to challenge but fell away to 208 all out. It was a tough loss as we played some good cricket. Sometimes you have to hold your hands up and say well played to the opposition. Over the four days they deserved the win.

There isn't much rest for the lads now with the T20 starting on Friday. It's a quick switch around for the Championship and it will test us. Leicestershire are first up and they are a strong T20 team with a good record. It was disappointing to lose, but the games come thick and fast now and we will have to assess today later. For now the focus moves on to Friday night.

LV= County Championship Division Two
Game 4 at Emirates Old Trafford, 10-13 May

Gloucestershire 388 (Dent 116, Jarvis 4-121,
Siddle 3-55) & 275-9 dec (Marshall 92,
Handscomb 76, Siddle 4-39)
Lancashire 364 (Horton 168, Prince 57, Norwell
4-95) & 208 (Petersen 63, Davies 58,
Miles 4-58, Payne 3-31)

Gloucestershire won by 91 runs

A century by Chris Dent helped ensure that Gloucestershire enjoyed the better of the opening day but Lancashire's bowlers hit back with four wickets over the final 11 overs to leave the visitors on 322-7 at the close. They added 66 the following morning to reach 388 but Paul Horton led Lancashire's reply with his highest score at Old Trafford, adding 134 with Ashwell Prince, on his way to an excellent 168 out of a total of 364.

Gloucestershire then batted themselves into a good position with a partnership of 134 between Hamish Marshall (92) and Peter Handscomb (76) the mainstay of their 275-9 declared despite four wickets from Peter Siddle in his last match before joining up with Australia.

Set exactly 300 to win from 70 overs, Lancashire slumped to 22–4 before a fifth wicket alliance between Alviro Petersen and Alex Davies of 118 runs in 24 overs revived Red Rose hopes. Once the pair fell either side of tea, Gloucestershire pushed home their advantage to run out winners by 91 runs.

14th May

IT'S BEEN a rest day for the lads today. Players vary how they use these days, some play golf while others enjoy time at home or some just sleep! For me it was back to Old Trafford with Sam. As the physio he rarely gets a day off because someone always seems to have a niggle of some sort. A bit of walking and running was on offer, gradually trying to build up my pace to somewhere near full intensity. Happily things seemed to be moving in the right direction. He mentioned the prospect of going to the Championship game at Leicester next week to continue my recovery with him, another positive sign.

15th May

FRIDAY NIGHT Live is here! T20 is increasingly becoming the most popular format of the game. Worldwide appeal and playing opportunities certainly capture the imagination of players. The chance to earn a lot of money is also a factor, especially the lure of the IPL.

Our campaign starts against Leicester tonight and with no Peter Siddle available we head into tonight's game with no overseas player. It's not a major problem-with the squad we have I'm sure we will be fine. Great to see big George Edwards make his debut tonight and get four wickets. He signed from Surrey during the winter and impressed in pre-season. Crofty played a blinder of a knock as we chased down 140. He's been a consistent player across all forms now for many years and hopefully higher honours beckon for him. It was great to start with a win. The crowd were fantastic on what was a slightly chilly night. Fingers crossed some warm weather arrives for these fixtures!

It was sad to say goodbye to Kyle Hogg last year. He was a massive loss for us having to retire due to his bad back. He always managed to hit a nagging line and length consistently and was Glenn McGrath-like in that respect. Tonight the club are holding a dinner to remember his career and celebrate the fine player he was. All the boys headed over after the game, and with a win in the bag it made the night extra special-especially with Andrew Flintoff, Peter Moores and Jimmy Anderson all there for Hoggy too.

NatWest T20 Blast
Game 1 at Emirates Old Trafford, 15 May

Leics Foxes 131-7 (15 overs, O'Brien 47, Edwards 4-20) Lancashire Lightning 142-5 (15 overs, Croft 70*)

Lancashire Lightning won by 5 wickets (D/L Method)

Steven Croft drew on all his 100-plus T20 game experience to lead Lancashire Lightning to a thrilling victory off the final ball against Leicestershire Foxes.

With two runs required, Croft cut the final ball away for four to seal a five-wicket Duckworth-Lewis victory after rescuing the side from a perilous 57-4 at the start of the 8th over with the help of Alex Davies, the pair adding 74 runs across seven action-packed overs. With ten required off the final over Croft drove the third ball off Ben Raine for 4 and square cut the last ball to clinch the win, finishing 70 not out from just 39 balls.

Earlier Ned Eckersley and Kevin O'Brien raced away with a barrage of sixes to take the Foxes to 63-1 in the sixth over and it took a combined effort by the Lancashire spin attack of Stephen Parry, Arron Lilley and Croft, to stem the flow of runs before rain intervened with Leicestershire 105-2 two balls into the 12th over. With the game shortened to 15 overs per side, the Foxes lost their way on the resumption with George Edwards, on his Red Rose debut, claiming four wickets including the key wicket O'Brien, as the visitors rather stumbled their way to 131-7, a total well below what they would have anticipated earlier.

16th May

OFF TO Leicester today, with the Championship game starting tomorrow. The games keep coming thick and fast and following last week's loss a win here is a 'must' to keep up this early season momentum. With no Peter Siddle, one of our bowlers will have to step up. It's tough to replace someone like that but, with the strength in depth we have, I'm sure whoever is chosen will hold their own.

My back was feeling good today and I was quite excited packing my kit before I left. Sad I know, but to me it was one step closer to playing again which is the thing I love the most. I knew I was going to find it hard to watch this week but being part of it felt so much better.

17th May

WHERE'S THE pitch?? Turning up at Grace Road it was tough to pick out the pitch from the outfield! It was bright green and fairly firm. A few team changes occurred with Karl Brown coming in for the injured Luis Reece and Nathan Buck came in to play against his former county, having left Leicestershire at the end of last season.

We got stuck in after losing the toss, with Browny and Horts battling to 40 before Browny got a good one off McKay that just held in the pitch. It was a crucial partnership, after being put in, as it settled the changing room. After that we had some mini partnerships that all helped to move the total along. Horts continued his good form with a fluent 70, and finishing the day on 350-6 was massive. To achieve that total after being put in was a testament to our batters. Crofty finished 98 not out, a true captain's knock, and I was gutted he couldn't get his hundred today but I'm sure he will finish it tomorrow.

Strapping on my pads today a few nerves hit me because the last time I had a bat, my back went into spasm. We started with a few simple underarm deliveries. Mundane yes, but doing the boring things will make you a better player. It was a giant leap forward in my recovery. Sam finished me off with a fitness circuit on the outfield at tea. It was a short sharp 20-minute blast which left me gasping for air. On the back of this we chatted about bowling tomorrow, another big step forward.

18th May

HAD THE pleasure of meeting Sam in the gym at 6.15am for a morning circuit! The initial shock of my alarm was soon a distant memory as I was pouring sweat out in the gym. I came out feeling refreshed though and ready to push on with my cricket activities.

We all gathered together in the morning to re-focus on the day at hand. With a good first innings score on the board it was imperative we backed it up with the ball first up. At 11.15 the lads congregated on the balcony to celebrate Crofty's hundred. It was a knock that showed great fight and we certainly needed it. We were soon bowled out only adding 13 to our overnight total. A big opening session with the ball was needed, and Jarv struck early. He's had a terrific start so far, coming back strong from last year. Hopefully he can maintain that throughout the season. We didn't bowl as well as we could, but still managed to pick up wickets at regular intervals. They were scoring at a good lick but the poles certainly swayed the day our way. Leicester finished on 195-6 as we held a firm grip on the game. With some poor weather in prospect over the next few days we need tomorrow to be a big day.

I managed to get six overs out in the nets as well, albeit off three steps, but it felt good to turn my arm over. I also strapped the pads on again today and faced the bowling machine. We worked at a good pace and Sam tested everything. All the mental rehearsal drills seem to have paid off and I felt in great nick.

19th May

WE MANAGED to bowl Leicester out for 249 to give us a lead of 119 with Jarv finishing with five wickets-another performance to build on. Mark Cosgrove their overseas batsman managed to frustrate us for a while with his slightly unorthodox, but highly effective, method of batting. Only 30 overs were possible today due to rain as we ended on 39-2, but with a good lead. The pitch is showing signs of uneven bounce and continues to offer movement, so a win looks possible as long as the rain stays away.

With the day being called off early, Sam and I went across to the indoor school to do some more work. It was about getting volume in now. I had also been pencilled in to play in a second team game. I wanted to feel a hundred percent right before I came back though. We had the ground to ourselves, and in the sweeping rain Sam put me physically through my paces with some agility work combined with speed work. It left my legs feeling spent!

20th May

WITH A lead of 158 runs coming into today it was clear what we had to do. There is some rain forecast that could hamper us but hopefully it will stay away. Knowing when to declare is the hardest part. With a lead of 322 we declared in the afternoon session. Ashwell held us together with a solid 76 not out and young Davo (Alex Davies) scored a run-a-ball fifty at the end to give us some impetus. We felt 60 overs were enough to bowl out Leicester and didn't think they would have a go at chasing the score down. On this pitch it would have been a great effort. It was all irrelevant in the end. Bails (Tom Bailey) returned figures of 5-12 off 9 overs-a match winning spell. He ripped the heart out of Leicester who crumbled to 78 all out. It was a great win for us on a tough pitch. The momentum was moving us forward in the Championship with each win bringing us closer to the title and promotion.

For me the week had been a great success. Sam passed me fit to play in the second team the following week. It had been a tough few weeks, but all worthwhile knowing I was going to be playing again.

LV= County Championship Division Two
Game 5 at Leicester, 17-20 May

Lancashire 368 (Croft 102, Horton 70)
& 203-5 (Prince 76*, Davies 54)
Leicestershire 249 (Cosgrove 79, Jarvis 5-69,
Buck 3-64) & 78 (Bailey 5-12)

Lancashire won by 244 runs

Half-centuries from Paul Horton and Steven Croft contributed to Lancashire's impressive 356-9 after being put in on the opening day at Grace Road in bowler-friendly conditions. Horton continued his good form with 70, sharing 97 for the third wicket with Ashwell Prince, while later in the day Croft added 73 for the sixth wicket with Jordan Clark and 77 for the eighth with Nathan Buck. Croft completed his century the following morning, being the last man out for 102 in Lancashire's 368.

Leicestershire struggled to 195-6 on a rain-hit second day with Mark Cosgrove's 79 the mainstay of the home side's reply. Further rain on day three meant it was approaching 6pm when the Foxes were eventually all out for 249, with Kyle Jarvis claiming yet another five-wicket haul and Buck taking three wickets on his return to his former county.

Prince hit an unbeaten 76 and Alex Davies a rapid 54 as Lancashire declared on 203-5 soon after lunch on the final day, setting Leicestershire a target of 323 in 59 overs. They never got close, thanks to a stunning bowling performance by Tom Bailey who blew the home side away with 5-11 in 9 overs. Bailey took five of the first seven wickets to fall as the Foxes were reduced to 29-7 inside 15 overs before they were later bowled out for 78 as Lancashire ran out winners by 244 runs.

21st May

YOU KNOW summer is here when the first Test Match arrives. England are hosting New Zealand for a two-match series. After drawing in the West Indies I'm sure they will be keen to get going at Lord's. The pitch looks pretty green so hopefully this will mean good pace throughout the Test. Great to see Adam Lyth making his debut. He has performed consistently over the last few seasons and thoroughly earned his place (even if he is a Yorkshireman!). It certainly was good viewing after losing early wickets. Stokes played a blinder of an innings. To play like that in conditions favouring swing bowling, of which New Zealand have a couple of high-class exponents, showed great technique and courage. I hope this sets the tone for the summer. If so, it's going to be great viewing.

Back to us. The lads are preparing for the T20 at Durham tomorrow while for me a lot of the work has been done. It's a case of working hard and keeping fit and strong in my core. The second team game on Monday can't come quick enough.

22nd May

NOT OUR greatest night. Durham can be tough opponents; they blow hot and cold in this competition and you're never quite sure what you're going to get. Tonight they turned up. With so many dangerous ball strikers you have to be right on top of your game. Mark Stoneman provided the foundation with a good 57 and we never really got going chasing 156 for victory. Ashwell carried his form into the tournament scoring a breath-taking 78 from 51 balls. Unfortunately we didn't quite get there. It's a long group stage and although early wins are key, it's not the end of the world losing one.

I had a good net prior to the lads arriving. My game felt really good although I was still a little nervy running in to bowl. Building confidence in your body is key when returning from injury.

NatWest T20 Blast
Game 2 at Emirates Old Trafford, 22 May

Durham Jets 155 all out (19.4 overs,
Stoneman 57, Lilley 2-18, Bailey 2-26)
Lancashire Lightning 139-9
(20 overs, Prince 78, Arshad 2-9)

Durham Jets won by 16 runs

Lancashire Lightning fell to a 16-run defeat against Durham Jets, despite the best efforts of Ashwell Prince in an entertaining encounter. The South African left-hander posted his highest ever T20 innings, with 78 off 51 balls, to underpin the Lightning's attempt to chase down their 156 target, but his run out in the 19th over with 24 runs required from 11 balls, effectively ended Lancashire's hopes. Prince's dismissal was the first of four wickets to fall in six balls from the 19th over as the Red Rose lower order perished hitting out valiantly, but unsuccessfully, to finish on 139-9. The result itself however, was anything but a foregone conclusion until those late wickets.

Earlier Durham were well set to post a big total from a position of 105-2 at the start of the 12th over, but the spin pair of Stephen Parry and Arron Lilley helped pull the Lightning back in to the game. Lilley, in particular, wheeled away to great effect to help stall the visitors' innings with 2-18 from his four overs. His dismissal of Paul Collingwood and then Stoneman, stumped for a well-made 57 from 38 balls two overs later, started a clatter of wickets as Durham attempted, but failed, to hit out to any great effect over the final part of their innings, with just 51 runs coming from the final 52 balls, to finish on 155 all out.

23rd May

THE TEST Match is moving along well and it certainly has captured the public's imagination. England are going to have to play well over the next few days to get anything from the game. Alastair Cook looked good today. If he can kick on and get a big one tomorrow it could be key. If he bats for the majority of the day, the others can play around him at their own tempo. It does look like we are staring down the barrel a little bit though. I'm still holding firm on my prediction I made earlier. It's going to be a successful summer.

24th May

THE WHITES are washed and ironed, the training kit sorted and spikes tightened. Holly wished me good luck as I left. She could tell I was nervous. I've been checking the forecast for the last week praying that there's no rain about. Driving down to Coventry, I couldn't help but get a little excited at the thought of playing again even though it had to be in a controlled manner. I could only bowl four-over spells with a total limit of three spells. Nothing epic, but a start. You can do all the running you want to get fit but there's nothing quite like bowling. I had forgotten about being captain for the week, the idea of playing had taken over. My body felt good and my back strong. Back to playing at last!

25th May

GAME DAY and I must admit I was pretty nervous. Trusting your body again can take time after an injury. Rooster (Dave Roberts, LCCC Head Physiotherapist) had come down to make sure I was fully prepared going into the game. Warming up, I gradually eased my way into it. I lost the toss, which turned out to be a good thing as we weren't quite sure what to do and, after being put in, to declare on 333-7 was a great effort.

I came in at number 4 and if I'm being honest was probably plum lbw first ball after I missed a full toss! I managed to battle my way to 32, trying to find some rhythm and timing. Technique-wise I felt good. My feet were moving well but my fluency wasn't quite there. Getting into the ball was tough early on. All in all it was a good day for both the team and myself.

After a stop-start beginning to my season I was ready to kick on and get back playing. I was potentially aiming for the Headingley T20 clash against Yorkshire. What a comeback game! I can't look too far ahead though as this week is crucial to my progression. My back stiffened up quite a lot at the end of play, and this left a few doubts in my head, but it was just soreness from being back on the park. The real test will come tomorrow with the bowling.

Not a bad result in the Test Match. Stokes' knock was something else-the dual between him and Southee was great viewing. You can't forget Cook's knock either. He held the innings together allowing the likes of Stokes to play their way around him. The England team deserve that win after the stick they have copped recently.

26th May

TODAY WAS the day I was most nervous about. Bowling. My action is pretty simple so getting back to a rhythm wasn't too bad. Getting back to being one hundred percent is the hardest thing. Running in I was thinking 'be careful, don't go too hard'. This then reflected in my bowling. I got through eight overs taking 1-33. I bowled indifferently-but it was a start. The first spell was the hardest-getting over the fear factor-but the lads were supportive as always, backing me the whole way.

It was a great chance for me to see some of our younger bowlers in action. Saqib Mahmood bowled with great pace and control for his three wickets and looked a real talent. The day ended well, we were 200 runs to the good with six wickets left. I was nervous today and the thought of my back going again did cross my mind. Getting through a day in the field has been a massive boost, but I will know more in the morning.

27th May

PART OF my routine every morning is getting in the pool. I've done it every morning for the past five years in an effort to prevent injury. It does have a lot of benefits, and although I've suffered a few injuries I do feel it's helped me. I needed it this morning! My back was stiff. After a good thirty minutes of stretching and swimming I felt it easing.

A big feature of second team cricket is playing three-day games. A result generally has to be set up through declarations that will enable a last day run chase. We set Warwickshire 312 in 60 overs, something achievable on a good pitch and a small ground. I did find this hard, as I just wanted to bowl a spell with as little stress as possible. The game itself turned out to be a thriller. They needed two runs to win from the last ball but could only manage a single. Rob Jones, one of our young scholarship players, produced a devastating bit of cricket throwing the stumps down from the boundary to leave the game drawn with the scores level, Warwickshire having two wickets left.

It had been a great few days for the team and myself. For me it was the first step back to playing and captaining Lancashire. We have two second team T20 games tomorrow which will certainly test my back! The Championship game at Southport also finished today. What a win! When two batters like Alviro and Ashwell get going it's tough to stop them. Chuffed too for Arron Lilley taking his first five-wicket haul, he's been impressive this year.

LV= County Championship Division Two
Game 6 at Southport, 24-27 May

Derbyshire 370 (Godleman 75, Slater 69,
Amla 69, Jarvis 4-132, Bailey 3-73)
& 166 (Slater 58, Lilley 5-23, Kerrigan 4-80)
Lancashire 551 (Prince 230, Petersen 113,
Lilley 63, Taylor 4-113)

Lancashire won by an innings and 15 runs

While Tom was making his comeback with the second team, Lancashire were making their first visit to Southport for two years. Derbyshire made a flying start after winning the toss, with openers Billy Godleman and Billy Slater sharing a 141-run partnership, but the Lancashire attack hit back well to take nine wickets before the close of the first day. Both batsmen departed early in the afternoon session with Slater edging Tom Bailey to slip for 69 and Godleman cutting Kyle Jarvis to gully for 75. Bailey ended a third-wicket stand of 83 when Chesney Hughes edged behind just before tea and Simon Kerrigan took two in two straight after the break to leave the visitors on 257-5. Lancashire enjoyed further success just before the close as three wickets fell for seven runs in 13 balls, with Jarvis getting the prize wicket of Hashim Amla, bowled for 69.

Matt Critchley hit out to make 41 and take Derbyshire to 370 all out on the second morning, but centuries by Ashwell Prince and Alviro Petersen dominated the remainder of the day which Lancashire finished strongly on 348-4. Prince continued his outstanding form to produce another batting masterclass while Petersen was in equally devastating mood during the afternoon, making 113 before edging behind off Taylor. Their partnership of 258 was a record for the 3rd wicket against Derbyshire and also the highest first-class partnership at Southport.

Prince was still there at the close on 156 and he moved through the gears on day three in going to his double-century. He added 78 with Jordan Clark for the 6th wicket and 81 with Arron Lilley before his 7 hour 40 minute innings came to an end at 230 when he pulled Critchley to short mid-wicket with Lancashire 523-7. Lilley went on to make 63-his maiden first-class fifty-as Lancashire ended on 551, the highest first-class score at this ground.

A 98-run partnership between Slater and Hughes ensured a good start to Derbyshire's second innings, but Lilley and Simon Kerrigan both took a late wicket apiece to make the score 123-3 by the close. The pair went on to rout the visitors before lunch on the fourth morning with some outstanding spin bowling. Lilley finished with 5-23, his first five-wicket haul, and Kerrigan 4-80 as they bowled unchanged from the start of the day. Derbyshire lost their last seven wickets for 43 runs in 36 overs, to lose by an innings and 15 runs as Lancashire made it four wins out of six to increase their lead at the top of the Division Two table.

28th May

T20 IS always fun, especially batting. However you play two games in the day in the second team which is draining, especially if you field back to back which we did. During the first innings of the day, I dived to get in going for a quick single and jarred my back! It was probably a stupid mistake but a natural reaction nevertheless. I just did it without thinking. We got to 185 off our 20 overs and managed to restrict Warwicks to 175-a great effort on the tiny ground at Walmley-and the boys bowled magnificently. My back was giving me a little bit of 'jip' though. I was trying to play through it, hoping it would go away.

The second game was very one-sided. We bowled them out for 90 and knocked them off inside 10 overs with Liam Livingstone showing his ball striking ability with a 50 from 20 balls. I decided not to bowl in this game as my back was still sore. Stupidly I was throwing myself around in the field. I find it hard to just let the ball go and have to give a hundred percent. It has been tough week playing-wise. My body certainly knows about it and I'm looking forward to a rest.

29th May

THE BACK feels okay today, a little stiff from the past few days but not too bad. The weather is top-draw today and perfect for golf. After asking Sam if I could play his response was short and sweet. Well not too sweet! The pool was on my list of things to do, and a nice long soak to help the joints in my back relax was just what I needed.

The lads were on the box tonight in the T20. Derbyshire have made some great signings with Hashim Amla and Dilshan two of the best batters in the world, so it's going to be a tough game. We never really got going and found our way to 127. The one-day pitches at Derby can be belters, but just from watching on the TV it looked different to the usual ones. The bounce seemed a little indifferent, not allowing free-flowing play. Dilshan and Amla certainly showed their class in the run chase. They raced to 90 off 10 overs, putting on a masterclass of batting. At times like these you have to say fair enough, well played. We nearly dragged it back late on, but they knocked the score off in the 18th over with five wickets down. I guess it was fairly comfortable in the end but we made them sweat!

NatWest T20 Blast
Game 3 at Derby, 29 May

Lancashire Lightning 127-9 (20 overs,
Davies 41, White 3-21)
Derbyshire Falcons 128-5 (17.4 overs, Amla 51)

Derbyshire Falcons won by 5 wickets

A top order batting collapse cost Lancashire the chance of a second T20 win as they fell to a five-wicket defeat against Derbyshire Falcons. Having been invited to bat first, the Lightning fell from 12-0 in the third over to 90-8 after 17. Former Red Rose bowler Wayne White struck with only his fourth ball in the fifth over when he bowled Karl Brown, leaving the score at 28-2, and he finished with 3-21 from his four overs. Lancashire's 127-9 saw only Brown with 10, Paul Horton with 20 and Alex Davies (41 off 26 balls) make it into double figures.

Experienced internationals Hashim Amla and Tillakaratne Dilshan then shared 93 in 10.3 overs to anchor the chase, a Derbyshire record for the first wicket in Twenty20 matches against Lancashire. Amla top-scored with 51 off 38 balls and Dilshan added 38 off 33. Jordan Clark struck twice for the Lightning to finish with 2-30 from four and debutant James Faulkner 1-31 from four as Derbyshire won with 14 balls to spare.

30th May

A LAZY day today. Washed the whites in preparation for next week's second team game at Derby and treated Holly to some dinner. I need to keep resting my back in-between playing and not playing. This will then help when it comes to game time. Also it's nice just to spend some time at home with your wife because you can end up being away a lot during the season.

31st May

THE LADS started at the Oval today, the one ground I'm yet to play at in my ten years of playing. Quite a strange fact given I've played for so long. Kevin Pietersen is making his return after injury in a bid to get himself back in the England team. There is no questioning his record as a player. He is one of the best players of this generation. If he plays again for England then we, as fans, will be lucky. I do feel that they will back the players they have at the moment though. More rain led to an early close with Surrey finishing on 145-4. You could say it was in the balance. Two quick wickets for us in the morning and we could roll them over. One good partnership for them and they could go on to build a big score.

I picked Stephen Parry up and we made our way to Derby for this week's second team games. I played all my junior cricket with 'Pazza' so it has been great see him go on to represent his country at the highest level, something I'm sure he is rightly proud about.

JUNE

Rehab and recovery

Watching brief: a regular event in my season

1st June

UP AND about early today. Got the pool done and breakfast down early. After the confidence of last week, and a good warm up, I felt great. The second eleven championship game is being played at Denby and I won the toss this time and decided to bowl not knowing how the pitch would play. Big mistake. It was pretty flat with a little bit of swing but slow! Showers were forecast throughout the day meaning the cricket would be broken up.

I came on to bowl after 10 overs, got a wicket in my second over, and my body felt strong; as good as it has done for a while to be honest. Then a shower arrived, forcing us off for 40 minutes. Not great timing, but nothing major. It soon passed through allowing play to resume shortly afterwards. Nice and loose I ran in to bowl, and there was no reaction from the first ball which always good after a break. Walking back to my mark, I was think "top, go off, knick him off" this is the motto I use before most balls.

Jumping and gathering at the return crease during the second delivery, I felt a sharp sudden pain in my back. My action collapsed and the ball nearly ended up at fine leg. It didn't feel great walking back to my mark and I knew something wasn't quite right. Attempting to get through it I set off to bowl the next delivery. Two strides in I knew it. "Bollocks!" I shouted. The pain returned with an instant, stabbing, sensation in my lower back. I threw the ball to 'Paz' who finished my over. As I made my way off I couldn't hide my frustration. I screamed into my jumper. The emotions running through my body were all negative. I could feel it stiffening up and I knew what was coming.

I saw their physio who gave me some tablets and did what he could. All that hard work and waiting round for what? I was gutted. I got on the phone to Sam, explained the situation, and then it was off to the scanner! My back was seriously stiffening up; it was starting to shift again.

I got to the scanner as quickly as possible. I'm on first name terms there now with the staff and I'm surprised they haven't offered me a loyalty card! As I lay in the scanner, the monotonous sounds of the machine in the background, I drifted into an almost hypnotic state. I knew it was going to mean a spell out again. How serious it was, or the length of time out, is still unknown but my gut feel wasn't great. After the scan I drove home and just lay on the couch staring out the window. There was no frustration or anger, just disappointment. I had been looking forward to this season so much. I was keen to back up last year and the chance to be captain made it so much more exciting. Back to square one I guess!

2nd June

THE RESULTS of the scan are expected back today, and until then it's a waiting game for me. I kept thinking over in my head if I'd done everything I could yesterday to get ready to bowl. I couldn't think of anything I could have done differently. Maybe it was just one of those things.

I lay in bed following the score at the Oval via the radio and the second team via the internet. The two's had been washed out for the day which made it even more frustrating for me. At the Oval it sounded like a hard slog, and with a bit of bad weather around the lads seemed to be on and off. Jason Roy scored a quick hundred, typical of his style. For me it was back to the drugs; pain killers and anti-inflammatories was my diet. Between getting up for a toilet break and lying down the day passed by uneventfully!

3rd June

THE RESULTS are in, as the judges would say. It wasn't a shock to me when Sam told me the news. I was expecting it. The bulging disc in my back had become a little bit bigger, causing me to go into spasm. I had trained all winter with this and it's chose the summer to rear its head. We booked in to see the specialist again, to see if there were any other courses of action to take. I knew then it would be another lengthy spell on the side-lines.

It looked a tough day at the Oval. With all the time lost to the weather a draw was probably inevitable. It was great to see James Faulkner, our new overseas player, come in and make an immediate impact, scoring his maiden first-class hundred. It came at an important time too with the game in the balance. Come the end of the season I wouldn't be surprised if Surrey and ourselves are in contention for getting promoted. They certainly have a lot of talent in their squad capable of winning games. They may struggle winning games at the Oval due to the nature of the pitch.

On a personal note it has been a disappointing day. Keeping a positive mind is crucial now.

LV= County Championship Division Two
Game 7 at the Oval, 31 May-3 June

Surrey 448 (Roy 143, Davies 86, Jarvis 4-118, Bailey 3-101) & 186-0 (Burns 110*, Ansari 66*)
Lancashire 429 (Faulkner 121, Clark 63)

Match Drawn

Play started late at 3pm on the opening day but in the 46 overs possible Kyle Jarvis struck twice, including getting Kevin Pietersen for 2, as Surrey, invited to bat first, slipped to 74-4 before responding with an unbroken fifth-wicket stand of 71 inside 13 overs between Steven Davies and Jason Roy. Tom Bailey claimed the early wicket of Rory Burns while Jordan Clark accounted for Kumar Sangakkara as the hosts closed on 145-4. Roy went on to compile an entertaining 143 off 166 balls on the second day, sharing 236 for the fifth wicket with Davies, who made 86, Surrey managed to build further through debutant fifty maker Ben Foakes, and they had reached 435-8 by the time bad light stopped play at 4.40pm before being bowled out for 448 early on the third morning.

Lancashire struggled to 108-6 in reply but were rescued by debutant James Faulkner and Clark during the second half of the day. Either side of tea, the pair shared 183 inside 47 overs to help pass the follow-on target of 299 and reach personal milestones along the way. Faulkner's 121 off 152 balls was his maiden first-class century and Clark's 63 off 142 was his maiden first-class fifty as the Red Rose closed on 342-8 from 89 overs. Lancashire then advanced their first innings to 429 all out on the final day before Surrey reached 186-0 from 61 overs in their second innings. The players shook hands on the draw at 4.50pm with left-hander Rory Burns unbeaten on 110 which meant Lancashire maintained their position at the top of Division Two table with a 31-point lead over Surrey.

4th June

THERE IS a lot of excitement around cricket right now. The Test series against New Zealand was entertaining to watch, and even though we lost the 2nd Test it was still gripping people in front of their televisions. With the upcoming Ashes series getting closer everyone is beginning to feel more confident. If England can win the one-day series they will carry some great momentum as they face the Aussies and with the nation behind them. I really hope they can prove a lot of people wrong. A lot of negative press has surrounded them since the West Indies tour.

On a domestic front one of the biggest games of the season has arrived. The Roses T20 clash. Tomorrow night Headingley will be bouncing. The forecast looks good and I'm sure the locals will provide a partisan atmosphere! These games are so much fun. Playing away from home has its ups and downs. Winning feels so much better, but fielding in front of the western terrace can be daunting. A few years ago I unfortunately mis-fielded one. The next 16 overs were interesting! It's all part of the experience; it's what you play the game for. The England players have been made available which will certainly provide an entertaining evening.

5th June

BEING INJURED is never good but sometimes it allows you to do things you wouldn't have been able to do if you were playing. Today I was able to attend my friend's wedding whereas if I was fit I wouldn't be able to go. I would rather have been playing but it was great to be there for his special day. However I did go missing for a while when the cricket came on. I found myself a quiet corner and thanks to modern technologies I was able to watch the game on my phone.

It looked like a great atmosphere and after Glenn Maxwell reverse swept the first ball of the match for six I'm sure it erupted! The pitch looked good and their international players showed their class. Joe Root and Gary Ballance played well to post 185. Headingley isn't the biggest ground and with our powerful middle order I backed us to chase the score. At the halfway stage I wasn't as confident. Yorkshire had bowled well and as soon as you fall behind the rate it can get tough chasing a big score.

Enter Jos Buttler. Having seen him play close-up for us last year it came as no surprise that he did what he did. Needing 17 off the last over was going to be tough; with Jos there it was possible. The quite corner I was in was no longer quiet! People had gathered round to watch. I couldn't help but scream when he hit the winning run. The celebration from the boys showed it all. It was a great advert for our game to the world. It was a great win for us as well. Having lost the last couple, it was important to start winning and getting over the line here could kick start a title-winning campaign. It was a great night to be part of Lancashire cricket and I'm sure the boys will remember it for a long time.

NatWest T20 Blast
Game 4 at Headingley, 5 June

Yorkshire Vikings 185-8 (20 overs, Root 55, Ballance 31, Faulkner 3-27) Lancashire Lightning 186-6 (20 overs, Buttler 71*, Prince 32, Maxwell 3-15)

Lancashire Lightning won by 4 wickets

Jos Buttler's blistering 71 not out off 35 balls stunned a sold-out Headingley to help Lancashire beat Yorkshire by four wickets in a last ball T20 Blast thriller.

Yorkshire's 185 for eight was underpinned by Joe Root's 55 off 39 balls with nine fours, uniting for a fourth-wicket 63 run stand with international colleague Gary Ballance, who made 31 off 18. But it was started by Glenn Maxwell reverse sweeping the first ball of the match for six over cover!

When Ashwell Prince was lbw to Maxwell for 31 during the 13th over of the Red Rose reply, Lancashire were 89-3 requiring 97 from the remaining 46 deliveries. Buttler, who came in at number four, started his assault during an important fourth-wicket stand with Steven Croft which added 52 runs off the next 28 balls.

Once Croft had departed, Buttler went on to overhaul a target of 45 off the last three overs, scoring 29 of the last 32 runs required. The Lightning needed 17 off the last over from Tim Bresnan and Buttler, who hit five fours and five sixes in his innings, struck the first three deliveries for 6,4,4, Two singles followed before Buttler got the one required off the final ball to clinch a thrilling victory.

6th June

HAVING MET with the specialist already, a few courses of action had been discussed. The doctor pointed out that the bulge had got bigger and I needed to rest and let the area settle. He explained how the body would naturally fix the area, but that it would take some time 6-8 weeks. This was a blow, but better than the other option - surgery! That would have been season-ender. The problem would have been fixed immediately, but my season would be over. For me it was a no-brainer. Even if I could get the last month in of cricket it would be worth it.

Between Sam, Rooster and Tom (Webster), our strength and conditioning coach, we developed a plan for me to return to cricket. Included in this was Pilates. By strengthening my core and the muscles around my disc it would create a more secure and stable base for me to move, hopefully solving my problem. The specialist agreed with this and thought it would be a great idea. The plan was to see Kim Roberts, Rooster's wife, who is a Pilates Coach a couple of times a week and combine this with lots of walking and light stretching. Having this programme in place made me feel good about the future. Today marked the starting point for the next few weeks. Yes, I was highly frustrated, but now with some direction, I could focus on the future.

7th June

AFTER LOSING to Gloucester at Old Trafford last month, the lads will be keen to get one back this week at Bristol. We are playing some good cricket at the moment and a win there will cement our place at the top of the table.

For me it was a day of getting ready! My rehab programme starts tomorrow. As I've said before it marks the start of my comeback. Every step I take now is towards playing again. I must admit it's not going to be taxing stuff but the gradual progression will mean my body adapts to the training. A little bit of walking isn't going to tire me out but will build the strength in my back, which is what I need.

Down in Gloucester it sounds like the pitch is bowler-friendly. Following the game briefly on the radio the weather sounded grim, and overcast conditions tend to help the bowlers. Our 275 all out may have seemed like not enough runs but Gloucester finishing on 15-2 proved that it was a bowler's day.

8th June

REHAB STARTS and my focus has now shifted from the game at Gloucester. Of course I'll keep track of what's going on down there but now it's time to concentrate on getting better.

A brisk walk this morning started me off. It got my body moving and the muscles in my back working. I met Rooster at the gym for my first swimming session. Over a coffee he explained how my programme would work and what was in store for me.

My first swimming session was pretty easy, a sort of introduction. Swimming can get a little tedious; the bottom of a swimming pool doesn't change much after ten lengths! This is where the mental discipline comes in. You have to be focused on what you want, and use that to drive you forward. If I was not one hundred percent committed to getting fit, then the programme would not work. I kept telling myself I would come back stronger. My day finished with a brisk walk round the block for twenty minutes. I tried to talk Holly into coming with me but she was having none of it!

9th June

THE GAME at Gloucester looks to be taking shape. Jarv took another four wickets in their first innings. He's on fire this year! Following our second-innings score, the 251 lead we have should be enough. Not as many as you would like, but something to bowl at. A great strength of ours is fighting back when we are up against it. I wouldn't say we were in trouble yet but we are certainly in a tough game. The first session will be crucial in the morning as I feel whoever wins it will win the game.

England started off the one-day series with a bang, 408! The game is going mad! With the new rules only allowing four men outside the circle there is always a boundary option for the batters. The way the players hit the ball these day though there could be all ten fielders out and it still wouldn't matter! Players are getting stronger and hitting it further and in all directions. Being a bowler is becoming less and less appealing. New Zealand are a strong one-day team, so to get an early win will boost the team moving through the series.

My back hasn't felt great today. During stages of rehab it can be a lonely road. You are on your own for a majority of the time. I've been trying a little to look to the future today to picture myself playing again. Little things like this make massive differences.

10th June

BOOM WHAT a win! Jarv has taken another five wicket-haul and has nine wickets in the game. It's great to see your team-mates come through after tough times. Kyle has worked hard at his game and he's now reaping the rewards. He has the ability to rip through a team in a session and today he did just that, bowling them out for 160. This win really does push us ever closer to promotion having won five of the 8 games in the first half of the Championship and we are sitting pretty at the top.

It was my first Pilates today. I've heard about the practice but never really taken the time to understand it. It uses a routine of exercises to improve your physical strength and flexibility. I don't think I've ever quite sweated like it! Kim put me through my paces, and you have to concentrate the whole time. Over time the aim is to develop a deeper understanding of your body and how it moves. I really enjoyed the session which came as a pleasant surprise. Driving home I was quietly confident that we had found a great way to solve my issues.

LV= County Championship Division Two
Game 8 at Bristol, 7-10 June

Lancashire 275 (Croft 65, Brown 57, Miles 5-61)
& 253 (Brown 56, Miles 5-60)
Gloucestershire 277 (Klinger 102,
Jones 88, Bailey 4-52, Jarvis 4-67)
& 160 (Dent 54, Jarvis 5-39)

Lancashire won by 91 runs

Half-centuries from Steven Croft with 65 and Karl Brown (57) helped Lancashire to a competitive 275 on the first day at Bristol. Glen Chapple came in for his first match of the season in place of Simon Kerrigan which meant Lancashire went into a Championship match without a specialist spinner for the first time since May 2012. Jordan Clark made 35 and Tom Bailey scored 30 while Chapple, batting at number eleven, walloped an unbeaten 29 off 13 balls.

The hosts slipped to 15-2 after ten overs of their reply at the close, and were in trouble at 72-5 on day two before a Michael Klinger century and 88 for Geraint Jones in a partnership of 167 for the sixth wicket helped them secure a first-innings lead of just two. Bailey finished with 4-52 and Jarvis 4-67, the pair taking four of Gloucestershire's last five wickets to fall for 38.

The wickets continued to fall on the third day as Lancashire moved from 14-0 overnight to 253 all out in their second innings on a pitch that had started to show signs of uneven bounce. Brown's patient 56 marked his second fifty of the match while Clark was the next best with 48. Gloucestershire new ball seamer Craig Miles claimed figures of 5-60 to go with his 5-61 in the first for his maiden ten-wicket match haul.

Chasing a target of 252, Gloucestershire closed on 24-1 with Jarvis striking in his first over to bowl Will Tavare. The Red Rose paceman took four wickets in 17 balls at a cost of only five runs during the early stages of the fourth afternoon as the home side collapsed from 113-2 to 119-7, with Bailey also striking in a run of five wickets in 29 balls for the concession of six runs. Jarvis went on to finish with 5-39 while James Faulkner also chipped in with an impressive 3-18 from 12 overs as Lancashire won comfortably in the end by 91 runs.

11th June

A WALKING day! Today I was alone with my thoughts; just me and the road. I walked around Didsbury where I live, taking in what was around me. I am very fortunate to play cricket. It has taken me to some amazing places and allowed me to make friendships that I wouldn't have otherwise made. It feel it's important never to take the game for granted as one day it will be over and someone else will be having their go. I love the game, and it has given me a lot back. It is times like these – when it's taken away from you - that you remember how much you love it and this thought alone was enough to motivate me.

12th June

FRIDAY NIGHT under the floodlights again at Old Trafford. Derbyshire are the visitors, and they will miss Hashim Amla who has finished his stint with them. Dilshan is still there, and he can certainly take the game away from you. It's great to see Saqib Mahmood make his debut. After a string of good performance in the second team he has got his chance, which he thoroughly deserves. He did ask me if T20 was around when I started playing. I politely let him know I'm not that old!

Big partnerships in T20 could be classed in the 80-100 bracket. Crofty and Faulk's 151 stand was incredible. At 50-3 after 7 overs, the game was in the balance. They both played out of their skin to get us to 201. From this position we were never losing. The boys bowled superbly and Saqib picked up a wicket at the end to cap his day off. We are very much alive in the T20 group but it looks like we will have to win the majority of our games to get a home quarter-final which would be ideal, although qualifying is all that really matters.

Earlier I had finished my swimming session, and it went slightly better from the last time although still not busting a lung. Time on your own can be good. You learn to be comfortable in your own company. This is a much needed trait in rehab training or you will lose the plot.

NatWest T20 Blast
Game 5 at Emirates Old Trafford, 12 June

Lancashire Lightning 201-3 (20 overs,
Croft 94*, Faulkner 47*)
Derbyshire Falcons 134 all out (18.2 overs,
Hughes 39, Parry 4-16)

Lancashire Lightning won by 67 runs

Steven Croft and James Faulkner blasted Lancashire to a memorable 67-run victory against Derbyshire Falcons with a record-breaking T20 partnership. The pair joined forces with the Lightning in a spot of bother at 50-3 midway through the 8th over. In fact the Lightning went six overs without hitting a boundary as the duo patiently rebuilt the innings, to steer Lancashire to 75-3 after 12 overs with little hint of the mayhem that was about to ensue. Faulkner started the fun with a six off the first ball of the 13th over from Tony Palladino, then smacked the next ball for 4, before Croft joined in with two further boundaries as 21 runs came from the over.

The fifty partnership arrived from 37 balls in the following over before Croft cut loose reaching his fifty from 30 balls to take the Lightning to 130-3 in the 16th over. The onslaught continued unabated with an astonishing 29 runs arriving from the 19th over bowled by the Falcons' overseas player Nathan Rimmington, and 20 from the final over from Wayne White. Croft finished on 94 not out from just 51 balls with two sixes and nine fours, a career-best in his 107th consecutive T20 match for Lancashire, while Faulkner made 47 from 30 balls with 3 sixes and 2 fours. The pair's 151-run partnership was Lancashire's highest for the 4th wicket in T20.

Derbyshire's reply faltered immediately as Durston edged his first, and Faulkner's second, delivery to Alex Davies behind the stumps. Tillakaratne Dilshan and Chesney Hughes steadied matters with an alliance of 36 runs in 4 overs, and Hughes and Billy Godleman added 42 inside 6 overs, but when Hughes perished for 39 at the start of the 11th over, Derbyshire's challenge faltered significantly at 79-3. Stephen Parry stepped in to seal the victory with a career-best 4-16 as the visitors subsided to 134 all out in the 19th over.

13th June

DIDN'T FEEL great today waking up and I could feel the week's work in my back. I have to be careful not to go too hard. Listening to my body, generally I can tell when I need to rest and when I think I can push on and work harder. Today was definitely a rest day. It was a good chance to get a few things done around the house. I've started to work on my CV too. It's something that has never really crossed my mind until now if I'm being honest. In the middle of putting it together I had a slight wobble when under previous work experience, 'barman' was all I had! Life after the game is always going to be a challenge. Exploring what you want to do can be tough, especially if cricket is all you've ever known. I'm still a little unsure of what I want to do myself.

14th June

THIS WEEK'S game against Leicestershire at Old Trafford is somewhat different from our previous ones. In an attempt to attract more people to come after work, the club have sought special permission from the ECB to start at 12.30. This would leave the last session finishing at 7.30 thus allowing more people to come to the last session. As an idea I love the concept, it is a brilliant idea. In reality it's tough to do in England-and Manchester for that matter.

After bowling Leicestershire out on the first day, the gloom descended and the floodlights took over from the natural light meaning the umpires could no longer stay in the middle. This makes the late start a problem as you are missing two hours of crucial cricket while others have played a full day. A win this week would keep us on top and losing time, while your rivals play, isn't going to help our case. This is where the concept falls down. With good weather then all would be well, but you are in the hands of the gods slightly. All that aside, we had a good day to roll them out for 207 to put us in the box seat. The forecast is good for tomorrow so hopefully conditions to bat will be easier than today.

My back felt good today; much better for the rest yesterday. A light walk was all that I needed. Again not much excitement, but it's (literally) small steps at the moment.

The ODI series is shaping up to be a cracker, with both teams wrestling to get the upper hand. New Zealand took a big step today chasing down 303 with relative ease. 300 has become the new 250 of the old format; it's no longer a par score.

15th June

IT'S CRACKING the flags here in Manchester, and no better way to spend it than watching another masterclass from Ashwell again. He is playing with so much confidence this year, it's a shock when he doesn't score runs at the moment. In full flow he can take any attack apart. By the end of the day we had built 100 plus lead. Browny played so well for his 96 that it was such a shame when he missed out on a deserved hundred. He has come into the team and taken his chance at the top of the order with both hands. All the lads where gutted for him today. Our opening stand of 91 set the tone for our innings, providing a solid platform for our middle order to come in and play positively. At 314-4 we are very much in control of the game.

I spent some of my day watching from the top of the double-decker stand at the Statham End. Since the redevelopment the ground has become a world-class venue. In the evening sun I watched as we took control of the game and the ground looked fantastic. I knew that really I just wanted to be out in the middle! As good as it was to watch from the stands there is no better place than the middle, but I know if I keep doing the simple things well, this will come.

16th June

A GREAT win for the boys and another century by Ashwell. He is in the form of his life. At the moment he can do no wrong; everything he touches turns to gold. To have someone playing like that in your team is a great asset. It just lifts everyone around you. Jarv took another five-wicket haul and it's even better when you have a couple of players on fire like that. He bowls such an attacking line and length. If there is anything in the pitch he will find it and, as you can see, take wickets. Arron (Lilley) backed him up with four wickets and he has shown a lot of improvement this year stemming from a winter abroad. It's great to see him do well. To win by an innings and 157 runs is massive! You won't get many bigger wins than that. We are really starting to build a lot of momentum in the four-day stuff. If we can carry it on to the T20 then I feel we have the team to go all the way.

It was an early start this morning for me with a walk around Didsbury. It was quite fresh which helped to wake me up! The afternoon involved a light core session helping to top up my Pilates sessions and my body feels pretty strong at the moment. I know it's early days, but the future looks good. Finding ways to beat the boredom is quite high at the moment!

LV= County Championship Division Two
Game 9 at Emirates Old Trafford, 14-16 June

Leicestershire 207 (Agathangelou 54, Bailey 4-69)
& 119 (Jarvis 5-44, Lilley 4-28)
Lancashire 483 (Prince 104, Brown 96,
Lilley 59, Horton 54, Naik 8-179)

Lancashire won by an innings and 157 runs

With an experimental late start, play started at 1.10pm after a 40 minute rain delay with the floodlights on in cloudy conditions that persisted throughout the day, so there was some surprise in Leicestershire's decision to bat. They possibly regretted it at 86-5 with Tom Bailey taking three wickets and Kyle Jarvis two, including his 50th of the season, but Andrea Agathangelou and Ben Raine then rallied to add 87 for the 6th wicket. Agathangelou's dismissal on 54, edging Bailey to Davies, started a collapse that saw the visitors' slump in spectacular fashion from 165-5 to 182-9 thanks chiefly to a hat-trick by James Faulkner. Leicestershire were soon all out for 207 before bad light prevent further play.

Paul Horton and Karl Brown responded with a 91-run alliance the following afternoon before 46 by Alviro Petersen helped the score along to 174-2. Brown had played some lovely shots in reaching 96 but his attempt to score his second first-class century ended in a heart-breaking fashion when a straight delivery from Raine kept low, trapping him lbw with the score 248-3 to break a partnership with Ashwell Prince that had realised 74 runs. Prince helped add 52 runs with Alex Davies going into the third day and a further 57 with Arron Lilley, and he went on to reach his 14th Red Rose century, making a delightful 104. Lilley played an entertaining innings of 59 from 41 balls as Lancashire hit out to race to 483 all out on the stroke of 'lunch' at 2.30pm, a lead of 276.

Jarvis struck early on the resumption with two wickets, Faulkner claimed another, and then just before 'tea' Leicestershire suffered a collapse as three wickets fell, all to Lilley, in 25 balls for the addition of just three runs to leave the visitors' reeling at 90-6. The end came quickly with two wickets in two balls by Jarvis soon after the interval and Lancashire wrapped up a three-day innings' victory at 6.45pm with further wickets for Lilley (4-28) and Jarvis (5-44).

17th June

WITH THE the lads resting today, I turned my attention to the one-day series against New Zealand. It is a must-win game for England. Looking at the two teams they are quite even. Both teams have players who can take the game away from you. This showed today with England's batsman coming to the fore to chase down 350 with six overs remaining. The standard throughout the series has been on another level. Hopefully this style of play will attract people to come and watch our 50-over tournament.

The simplicity of my rehab programme hit home today-walk at a brisk pace for 25 minutes, then rest. That's tough to cope with as an active person; you want to be out doing stuff. Don't tell Holly but even doing the hoovering seemed appealing! Rooster uses the term "you can't cheat time". This is so true. My back is only going to get better with time. How long that is we don't know, but I guess the phrase 'time heals all wounds' is very apt as well. It's tough to see the finish line at the moment, but I know it's out there.

18th June

WE HAVEN'T really got our T20 campaign up and running yet, a couple of losses have pegged us back a little bit. We have played some good cricket but not consistently. Worcestershire visit Old Trafford tonight and they are flying in this competition.

I felt a lot better today in my back. It's still early days, and you have ups and downs on the way back to full fitness, but days like today make you look forward to getting back on the park.

19th June

IT WAS a tough loss last night. I thought we did enough to win the game but didn't quite get over the line. You have to hand it to their lower order and to Cox who hit a 6 off the penultimate ball to the longest boundary on the ground to win it. You can't lay the blame anywhere, it was just one of those things. In any sport sometimes you just have to admire brilliance, and this was a brilliant match-winning shot. The competition is wide open at the moment. Everyone seems to be winning and losing, and if we can string a couple of wins together we will go a long way to qualifying.

I'm finding the Pilates exercises I started last week very beneficial. It works the muscles deep inside you; the ones that control and stabilise your movements. After only a few sessions I can feel the stability increasing while performing the exercises. I think this will be a common practice for the rest of my career now. If it keeps me fit and on then park then it's a no-brainer.

NatWest T20 Blast
Game 6 at Emirates Old Trafford, 18 June

Lancashire Lightning 163-5 (20 overs, Brown 42, Prince 33, Croft 31)
Worcs Rapids 164-8 (19.5 overs, Mitchell 53)

Worcs Rapids won by 2 wickets

Ben Cox was the Worcestershire hero as the Rapids wicketkeeper hit an unbeaten 22 to take his team to an unlikely two-wicket victory with one ball to spare in a dramatic finale. When Colin Munro was run out for 22 at the end of the 14th over and Daryl Mitchell departed for 53 at the start of the next, the visitors' on 108-4 still needed 56 to win. Cox and Brett D'Olivera added 37 runs from 20 deliveries before D'Olivera was run out by James Faulkner at the end of the 19th over. With seven required from the final over bowled by Faulkner, and then six needed from 2 balls, Cox hit the fifth delivery over the long-on boundary to clinch a memorable victory for the visitors.

It was a disappointing defeat for Lancashire, who had posted 163-5 from their 20 overs on the back of Karl Brown's 42 from 24 balls and good contributions from Steven Croft (31 off 25) and Ashwell Prince (33 from 28). After seven overs without a boundary, late order hitting by Croft, Faulkner, Alex Davies and Jordan Clark had helped add 61 from the final six overs of the innings as Lancashire set a challenging total.

20th June

ANOTHER TOUGH loss last night. I thought Faulks was going to see us home. He must have played out of his skin! Again we are so close to winning. A few little tweaks here and there and I'm convinced we will push for the trophy this year!

I have Saturday off to let my back recover from the week's work. I know it doesn't sound very stressful, and you may think I'm being lazy, but rest is crucial. Any physio or strength coach will tell you this. The rest period is when your body adapts to all the training you are doing. To pass a bit of the time I've taken to cooking. Trying to make pasta on your own, from scratch, is pretty tough. Holly looked at the final result and promptly rang the local take away for a pizza! I did feel a little hurt that she cast it off without even trying it, until I had some and realised why she did. I'm sure it will get better with practice.

NatWest T20 Blast
Game 7 at Northampton, 19 June

Northants Steelbacks 169-5 (20 overs,
Cobb 47, Parry 2-25)
Lancashire Lightning 165-8 (20 overs,
Faulkner 73, Davies 34, Azhar Ullah 3-28)

Northants Steelbacks won by 4 runs

Some memorable big-hitting from James Faulkner went unrewarded as Lancashire slipped to a four-run defeat in an enthralling game with Northants. Chasing a victory target of 170, the Lightning slipped to 55–4 after nine overs before Faulkner shared 89 inside nine overs for the fifth wicket with Alex Davies, who hit 34 off 24 balls. The Australian all-rounder smashed 73 off 44 balls, including three fours and four sixes, to take the target to 14 off the last over, bowled by Azhar Ullah. That became five off the last ball, only for the all-rounder to be caught and bowled.

Josh Cobb's 47 off 33 balls had led the way in Northants' 169-5 after they had been invited to bat. Cobb and Richard Levi started with a 67-run alliance off 7.4 overs before Stephen Parry got both openers in three balls on the way to figures of 2–25. The Steelbacks were pegged back by the spin of Parry, Arron Lilley and Steven Croft, only reaching 100-3 after 13 overs, but found late order impetus to post a challenging total with Alex Wakely hitting an unbeaten 36.

21st June

THE LADS had no game this week in the Championship. It has been a gruelling few months for them and a well-earned rest is required. We are pushing for promotion already and very close to turning it around in the T20. Sometimes it's good for the lads to get away. When you are on the road you are constantly with each other and a bit of time away can be crucial. You come back recharged and ready to go. The game this Thursday against Durham is going to be massive. We desperately need a win to kick-start our tournament.

25th June

IT'S BEEN an exciting few days with the lads around the ground. They have been training hard for these next two games. If we win tonight and tomorrow then I'm pretty confident we will qualify. I don't think there is a case for losing both, and one win will mean things are out of our hands and it's never nice when your destiny as a team is taken out of your own control.

My Pilates is coming on really well and Kim has been stepping it up each session. The control is becoming more consistent and practice a lot better. My back is also starting to feel the effects. The symptoms in my legs are easing off, allowing me to move more freely, but I still can't take any liberties. Ultimate focus is needed to maintain this progression forward-one act of stupidity could put me back weeks.

I settled in to watch our game on TV although I find it easier listening on the radio. Watching it live on the television certainly doesn't help stress levels! The Riverside can be a tricky place to play. Generally their one-day pitches are good and you can play your shots, but occasionally they can be more bowler-friendly. It's a massive ground when the boundaries are pushed back, and running between the wickets is crucial as boundaries can be hard to come by. This was evident tonight. Ashwell looked knackered coming off at the end! He had certainly run his fair share of two's, and he played a great knock seeing us home. I thought we did well to restrict them to 141 after the start they got. We kept taking wickets, which is crucial in restricting the opposition.

It's a massive win for us; we go in to tomorrow's game now full of confidence. There is no better thing than winning to build you up as a team. Last year's winners, Birmingham, are going well so far. They have managed to snap up Brendan McCullum who hasn't really fired yet this summer while playing for New Zealand. He can be a devastating batsman who we will need to get out early.

NatWest T20 Blast
Game 8 at Emirates Durham ICG, 25 June

Durham Jets 141 all out (19.5 overs,
Stoneman 51, Jarvis 3-24, Faulkner 3-27)
Lancashire Lightning 143-4 (18.1 overs, Prince 63*)

Lancashire Lightning won by 6 wickets

An outstanding bowling performance was at the heart of Lancashire's six-wicket victory against Durham. The Jets had raced to 72 in the first seven overs as Mark Stoneman, who top-scored with 51 off 29 balls, led the charge. Arron Lilley bowled Stoneman midway through the 11th over and Durham, 97-4, failed to score another boundary from this point. The spinners, Lilley, Stephen Parry and Steven Croft combined to take four wickets while Kyle Jarvis and James Faulkner claimed three apiece in bowling the home side out for 141.

Ashwell Prince anchored the Lightning reply with 63 and was still there when the winning runs arrived from the first ball of the 19th over. Karl Brown hit two sixes in his 17-ball innings of 26, and Faulkner did likewise with his 23 coming off 14 deliveries as the Lightning ran out comfortable six-wicket winners.

26th June

IT'S A massive game for us tonight. The Sky TV cameras are down to screen the game and there are a number of high quality performers on show. Faulkner, McCullum, Croft, Prince to name just a few. On the back of last night the boys are flying high. The Bears won the toss and elected to bat, and we probably would've also batted as the pitch looked good. They got off to a bit of a flyer, which was probably to be expected a little with the power they had up top. Clarky picked up the crucial wicket of McCullum with Crofty talking a superb catch running round from long-off to long-on. From there they steadily lost wickets ending up getting 137 off their 20 overs-a score we felt we could chase down. The pitch did change a little; it lost a lot of pace and the ball began to stick in the wicket. It suited their bowlers too, who like to take pace off the ball. Despite Livi's best efforts at the end, we fell one run shy. Gutted. We have come out on the wrong side of a couple of close games now. It's really frustrating as we are playing good cricket. Maybe we aren't putting it all together just yet. They did bowl well tonight in conditions that aided their attack so maybe we shouldn't be too hard on ourselves.

NatWest T20 Blast
Game 9 at Emirates Old Trafford, 26 June

Birmingham Bears 137-8 (20 overs,
Chopra 40, Porterfield 36, Parry 2-19, Croft 2-20)
Lancashire Lightning 136-8 (20 overs,
Faulkner 34, Gordon 4-20)

Birmingham Bears won by 1 run

Birmingham Bears won a pulsating T20 contest by one run in a low-scoring encounter at Old Trafford. Needing 17 off the final over, Liam Livingstone hit Ricky Gordon's second delivery for 4 and the fifth for 6 to leave three required from the final ball of the match. Sadly, for the Lightning, his fiercely struck drive went straight to mid-off and the one run scored left the Bears celebrating the narrowest of wins. It was Gordon who proved to be the Bears match winner, with a career-best 4-20 and crucially he only conceded 3 runs off the 19th over while taking two wickets.

Earlier Lancashire, chasing a target of 138, had recovered from 62-4 in the 12th over with a fifth wicket partnership of 39 in five overs between James Faulkner and Jordan Clark. Faulkner was Lancashire's main hope at this point with 34 from 25 balls, the Australian having pulled Patel for 6 just before Clark's dismissal. But when he lofted Gordon to Laurie Evans at long-off at the start of the 19th over, the Bears scented victory with Lancashire 119-6 needing 19 runs from 10 balls before Livingstone gave them a huge scare.

At the start of the game Steven Croft took a stunning catch, running 30 yards from long-off to get rid of the dangerous Brendan McCullum for 18 and break up an opening partnership of 49 inside six overs with Varun Chopra. Birmingham's total of 137-8 was due largely to the efforts of Chopra with 40 and Will Porterfield who made 36. The Bears only scored 67 from their final ten overs with boundaries a rarity. Steven Parry took 2-19 and Croft 2-21 from their four over stints to strangle the life out of the Bears innings on a wicket taking spin and where run-scoring was far from easy.

27th June

MY BACK seems to be getting better day by day at the moment. The core work I'm doing certainly seems to be paying off, but I still can't rush things. I feel like I could play right now but I know it would be the worst thing I could do. This is the hardest part. Today, I was out on my walk feeling great. I could have run-I wanted to run-but I have to be patient. It's a constant mental battle trying to hold yourself back from doing too much.

28th June

FOUR-DAY CRICKET returns tomorrow with Northants visiting Old Trafford and Alviro has a bit of a back issue and may not be fit. He will be a big loss. When injuries do occur then chances are created for other players. Someone will get a go this week who perhaps would not have before.

29th June

TODAY WAS the end of my season. Sometimes things happen that you can't control.

Getting out of bed this morning I felt what can only be described as an intense stabbing pain ripping down the side of my leg. It was agony. I couldn't sit still and I couldn't walk. I didn't know what had happened but knew it wasn't good. My whole left leg was on fire, and trying to walk was tough. I had to drag my leg along with me! Panic set in as I knew something serious was up, but had no idea what to do.

I got hold of Sam and he immediately performed some tests on me to assess the situation, followed by some painkillers. The tests he performed were the same ones the specialist had done previously. This time I couldn't even rock back onto my heel. All motor control in my front shin had gone.

They say the eyes tell a thousand words and Sam's were only saying one; trouble. He immediately arranged an appointment with the specialist and another scan for me. I knew deep down at that moment my season was done. This was a pain like nothing else I had encountered with my back.

I was gutted; really gutted. I had been looking forward to this season more than any. I genuinely believed I would play some cricket this year, and that I would get over this problem. All the hard work, the rehab, the mundane exercises felt like they were for nothing. Deep down I was hurting.

30th June

I'M FEELING pretty low today. The pain in my leg has settled a little bit, but the symptoms are still coming on strong. The control I have of my leg is disappearing quickly, I'm having to drag it along with me to get anywhere. I'm booked in to see the specialist on Friday and I'm pretty sure what he will say. The thought of having an operation is bad. The thought of having one on my back is even worse!

The game against Northants at Old Trafford has been tough. They have played well to get to 438 all out. Ben Duckett scored a solid hundred and he played positively throughout his innings. He's not the tallest man either and finding the right length can be tough as a bowler. We finished the day on 257-4 with Browny making 97. He grafted for hours to get there and was undone by a good bit of bowling. The way he's playing, it wouldn't surprise me if he got a monster score soon!

JULY

The worst of days, the best day

Pleased for Pazza: with the rest of the lads to see Stephen Parry receive his Lancashire Cap from Lancashire chairman Michael Cairns

1st July

WHERE IS this year going? I'm feeling extremely frustrated at the moment, but trying not to show it around the changing room. I've resigned myself now to the fact that an operation is going to be needed to solve this problem. If anything, I'm more relieved now. I just want it to be over so that I can move forward and start getting fit for next season. Can't believe I'm already looking forward to next season! There have been ups and downs, good days and bad days so far. What's keeping me sane is the thought of coming back stronger than before.

I've decided to stay away from the cricket today. I don't want to get in the way of the lads while they have to prepare for a big day. On the bright side if I do have to have an op there is plenty to watch on television this summer. I'll have a great excuse to watch the cricket all day!

2nd July

NOT A great night's sleep, my leg keeps playing up and any movement in my back just enrages it further. I can't wait to get this sorted. There's not a great deal I can do at the moment. I can't venture very far and sitting in a car is a no-go at the moment. I guess if I do have an operation it will be like this so I'd better get used to it!

Looks like the weather came to our aid today. We weren't quite at our best in this fixture, so to come away with a high-scoring draw is a plus. Northants are a strong team who will be pushing for promotion. We have probably dodged one today, with the rain coming at a good time. I'm sure though that there will be another time this season when it comes to thwart us chasing a victory. It's something you can't control, so it's really not worth worrying about at all.

LV= County Championship Division Two
Game 10 at Emirates Old Trafford, 29 June-2 July

Northants 438 (Duckett 134, Rossington 89,
Faulkner 4-63, Jarvis 3-122) & 283-9 dec
(Duckett 88, Kerrigan 3-94, Lilley 3-97)
Lancashire 308 (Brown 97, Prince 83, Davies 51)
& 206-7 (Brown 82, Horton 65)

Match Drawn

It was advantage Northamptonshire after the opening day as the visitors racked up 388-6 thanks to two century partnerships. The first between Ben Duckett, who made 134, and Alex Wakely (56) added 172 for the second wicket in the morning, and was followed by 142 for the fifth wicket between Adam Rossington and Richard Levi (57) in the afternoon. Rossington fell for 89 early on day two as Northants were bowled out for 438.

Lancashire replied with century partnerships of their own; 109 for the second wicket between Karl Brown and Alex Davies, who made 51, and 116 by Brown and Ashwell Prince for the third. Both Brown and Prince batted superbly, continuing their good form, and it was a surprise when they departed late in the day, Brown for 97 and Prince for 83, to leave the Red Rose on 257-4 at the close.

On the hottest July day ever recorded it was Lancashire who were left feeling the heat as Northants applied the pressure on the third day, bowling the home side out for 308 with the Red Rose losing their last five wickets for 29 runs in 56 balls. Duckett then made it a game to remember with an innings of 88 to help Northants reach 283-9 with their declaration setting Lancashire a victory target of 414 in 102 overs.

An opening partnership of 130 between Brown and Paul Horton gave Lancashire great encouragement throughout the final morning, but after the heat of the previous day showery weather threatened to intervene all day. After one interruption before lunch, Olly Stone hit back for Northants, bowling Horton for 65 in a spell of 3-9 and forcing Lancashire into a defensive mode. When Brown was out for 82, his fifth consecutive half-century, Lancashire had fallen to 179-5 and were in trouble soon afterwards at 206-7 with 35 overs left. However the rain returned at 3.30pm to end the game and force a draw.

3rd July

I SAW the specialist last night with Rooster and Sam and it wasn't good news. Within twenty seconds of looking at my scan he broke the news that I would need an operation. Deep down I was getting myself ready for the news, but that wasn't all of it. He explained the reality of the situation; that bowling may no longer be an option for me, especially in the four-day game.

He also the expressed the importance of my recovery, and that from now on I would have to look after my back extremely well. As he is compelled to by law, he explained all the complications and the chances of success. I just expected an operation to work if I'm being honest. I certainly didn't expect him to say there's a 1 in 20 chance it may not.

Coming out of the meeting we had a coffee. Rooster and Sam explained my options, and I suddenly broke down right there at the hospital. The thought of not being able to play again was horrific. All of a sudden worries that I'd never had entered my head. What are we going to do? Where am I going to work? Sam and Rooster calmed me and reassured me that the chances of success were high and that with a good recovery all will be well. I didn't know what to think.

Driving home I could have been anywhere. Every fear and doubt in my head just made the situation so much worse. Breaking the news to my wife Holly was tough, although she was a little relieved and was very positive in her approach. She looked at it from the angle of a fresh start. That finally it will be fixed and we can move on.

The Roses T20 is a massive day for the club. It's our biggest domestic game at Old Trafford and a packed house is certain. Missing these big games is horrendous.

And tonight's T20 fixture was an epic. We blew them away from the first over. Horts and Ashwell showed great intent and from there it continued. We amassed a score of 231 and everyone played their role perfectly. In the interval Browny said "he felt sorry for me that I couldn't bat on that pitch". It did look a belter and that showed in the Yorkshire innings. They had Finch and Maxwell who are two very dangerous customers. Even though we had a massive score it still wasn't safe with these two playing, but Pazza got both of them-Finch for 33 and Maxwell for 1. Their total of 202 was a brave effort, but it was always going to be a tough ask. It was a great win. Old Trafford was rocking and everyone went home happy.

NatWest T20 Blast
Game 10 at Emirates Old Trafford, 3 July

Lancashire Lightning 231-4 (20 overs,
Brown 69, Prince 59)
Yorkshire Vikings 202-8 (20 overs, Bresnan 51,
Gale 35, Finch 33, Parry 3-29, Lilley 3-31)

Lancashire Lightning won by 29 runs

Lancashire hit their highest ever T20 total to win a pulsating, entertaining, Roses match by 29 runs and keep their NatWest T20 Blast hopes very much alive. Paul Horton and Ashwell Prince made a lightning start, no pun intended, hitting 76 runs in an opening partnership off just 38 balls. Prince hit four sixes and three fours in making 59 from 30 balls, adding 32 in three overs with Karl Brown, before top edging Rich Pyrah to Johnny Bairstow from the last ball of the 10th over with Lancashire 104-2.

Brown launched a one-man blitz striking five fours and five sixes between the seventh and fifteenth overs in an innings that realised 69 runs from 35 balls. He went to his half-century from 25 balls after hitting Pyrah for three consecutive sixes in the 13th over which cost the bowler 27 runs, after an earlier three ball 6-4-6 sequence off Tim Bresnan in the 11th over. Then some good late order hitting carried the Red Rose to their record-breaking total of 231-4, also the most ever conceded by Yorkshire in T20.

Yorkshire replied powerfully with 63-0 from their six powerplay overs but Stephen Parry made a decisive double breakthrough in the seventh over, ending Aaron Finch's innings at 33 and four balls later accounting for the Vikings' other Australian overseas player, Glenn Maxwell for 1. Gale rallied his side, who reached the start of the tenth over still in contention on 88-2, but the Vikings captain was then run out for 35 by a direct hit from Arron Lilley, while Andrew Hodd went for a duck after striking Parry to Steven Croft in the deep. Once Bairstow was bowled by Croft for 26, the game was effectively over with Yorkshire 102-5 and needing 130 runs from 54 balls. Bresnan indulged in some spectacular hitting with 51 off 24 balls including five sixes, but the Vikings were too far back for it to affect the result as Lancashire ran out comfortable winners.

6th July

OPERATION DAY. Yesterday was spent preparing for today, packing my bag and generally panicking about today! Holly and I arrived at the hospital around 10am. I was due to go under the knife around midday which meant no eating from the previous night so I was starving. I just wanted to get it done so I could eat something! As nervous as I was, I knew that I was in the best possible hands for the surgery and aftercare.

My legs were tingling a lot today, probably aided by my nerves. I knew I was doing the right thing and that I would come out stronger on the other side. Then I was wheeled down to theatre, saying goodbye to Holly while my nerves built. The anaesthetist gave me a cocktail of drugs and I felt like I was floating. Then black. As you can probably understand I didn't remember the operation! Waking up, I didn't know where I was let alone that I had been having surgery.

Arriving back in my room I was greeted by the smile of Holly and food! Lots of food and although, by then I didn't really feel like eating, I managed to have some. Hol was brilliant, she looked after me all day. The nurses were amazing too and everything seemed to be going well.

Around 7pm the urge to go to the bathroom arrived. I was dreading this moment. I had to roll myself out of bed and in stages get to my feet. Feeling okay, I staggered to the toilet with the nurse pointing out the locations of the bars that I had to hold onto. Halfway through passing urine I blacked out, fainted, and fell into the shower. The next thing I knew I was back in bed with an oxygen mask on with everyone fussing around me. My first thought was that I had damaged my back again, which brought a wave of panic over me and probably didn't help the situation. Finally I calmed down, the doctor arrived to perform some tests, and all seemed to be fine again. It was a brief scare but everything was okay, thankfully!

9th July

I HAD to stay in a night longer than expected due to my fall. When the specialist gave me the all-clear I thought all my symptoms would just slowly ebb away, but if anything they are almost worse. Apparently this is to be expected as the nerve is repairing itself. Every little twinge I felt scared me. Things had gone well in the operation though and it is important that I don't rush things now. I have to do nothing; literally nothing. The specialist explained that the first 2-3 weeks are crucial. Mentally I have to stay positive; fighting it would only set the recovery back.

The one shining light from all of this is the Ashes has started at the perfect time! It will make lying in bed that little bit easier! Holly had set up the spare room with the computer at the end of the bed, a coffee table by my side and a selection of goodies to get me through the day! Good effort!

LV= County Championship Division Two
Game 11 at Emirates Old Trafford, 6-9 July

Lancashire 402-8 dec (Croft 122, Faulkner 68)
Essex 203 (Browne 105, Faulkner 5-39)
& following-on 168-3 (Browne 50)

Match Drawn

While Tom was recovering from his operation, Lancashire's players were enjoying the best of a rain-hit draw against Essex at Emirates Old Trafford.

A severely-truncated first day saw Lancashire close on 96-4, and the Red Rose were still batting at stumps on a shower-interrupted second day with Steven Croft 85 not out in a score of 257-5. The Red Rose stand-in skipper went on to post his second century of the season on the third day, making 122 and enjoying a sixth wicket partnership of 144 with James Faulkner that took Lancashire to 315-6 in the 86th over. Faulkner made 68, while Arron Lilley hit a six and five fours in a rapid 31-ball unbeaten innings of 40 in an eighth wicket alliance that added 55 runs from 6.4 overs in a frantic 30 minutes as the 110-over mark approached.

It allowed Croft to declare on 402-8, with Lancashire gaining a fifth batting point, and then watch his bowlers work their way successfully through the Essex line-up. Toby Lester, making his first-class debut, shared the new ball with Jarvis and made a sensational start taking a wicket with his tenth delivery, bowling Jaik Mickleburgh for 1. Lester also took a second wicket to make Essex 50-2 before being replaced by Faulkner and the Australian followed with a devastating burst of his own, taking 3-9 in four overs, to put Essex in trouble at 81-5. Nick Browne batted solidly to try and hold the innings together, the opener reaching his century on the fourth morning and finding support from James Foster, the pair adding 79 but crucially using up time, before being parted an hour into the final day.

Lilley took two wickets in two balls to wrap the Essex innings up for 203 moments before lunch, and although Croft enforced the follow-on, the visitors rallied to see the game out for a draw at 168-3.

10th July

I'M FEELING a lot better today in my back. I haven't had to do a great deal of moving, but there is a vast difference from a couple of days ago. Phil Scott, our former strength and conditioning coach, has lent me a book on meditation and the power of the mind to heal the body. It's a fascinating read and tells of accounts where people have literally thought themselves better. I'm going to give it a go. It can't do any harm, and it will also help me relax and cope with the pain which still feels strong in my leg. The shooting sensations keep flying up and down, and each time it's a little worrying. I keep having to tell myself everything is okay and that it's entirely normal. The truth is it feels as far from normal as possible!

While being able to watch the Ashes is great, after three days boredom has hit me at a new level. I realise how lucky I am now to be playing this game for a living, and how at times I may have taken it for granted. The game gives you so much, and when it's a taken away you soon realise how much you enjoy it. Keeping myself busy now is key. It's not often you are blessed with this much spare time in the summer. I need to use it wisely!

I see the rain at Old Trafford came to help Essex this time, just as it did for us in the previous game. The weather in Manchester can play a big part throughout the season; it tends to even itself out but can be highly frustrating. A high-scoring points draw was enough to keep us sitting pretty on top. A few more wins and you would like to think promotion will be secured.

NatWest T20 Blast
Game 11 at Leicester, 10 July

Lancashire Lightning 191-5 (20 overs, Horton 63, Brown 52, Croft 50)
Leics Foxes 151-8 (20 overs, Clark 3-41, Parry 2-29)

Lancashire Lightning won by 40 runs

Lancashire racked up another big score after being put in at Grace Road after Karl Brown and Paul Horton raced away with a second wicket partnership of 75 in nine overs. Brown scored his second fifty on the bounce with six fours and two sixes in his 34-ball 52 before being run out by a sharp piece of work by Mark Cosgrove from short cover at the start of the 12th over. Horton kept the scoreboard moving with 63 off 48 balls and shared a 91-run stand in eight overs for the third wicket with Steven Croft during the second half of the innings. Croft hit four fours and three sixes in his 50 off 25 to steer the Lightning to an imposing 191-5.

Leicestershire made a good start themselves with Mark Cosgrove and Ned Eckersley reaching 39-0 in the fifth, only for the latter to be bowled by Kyle Jarvis. Jordan Clark then had Cosgrove caught at cover and when Stephen Parry's first ball accounted for Ben Raine, caught at mid-on, three wickets had fallen in ten balls to leave the Foxes on 51-3. Pegged back, the home side started to struggle and when New Zealand all-rounder Grant Elliott hit Croft to deep backward square-leg to leave the score at 89-4 in the 12th over, the game was all but over. The Lightning attack dominated from that point as Leicestershire, needing 103 runs from 52 balls, fell well short on 151-8 as Lancashire clinched a sixth win from 11 games.

11th July

LAST NIGHT was a struggle. The pain in my legs was unbearable at times, which made sleeping tough, but I managed to drift off for a few hours. Waking up my back felt good and getting up and out of bed was getting easier-an encouraging sign!

A lot of my time is spent reading at the moment. As I can't get out the house, it's my form of escape. Psychology fascinates me a lot, especially on how it affects your performance and the way you perform. The book I'm reading explains a lot about your personality and how you can improve interacting and getting the best out of people and yourself. My mental state is important at the moment. Keeping positive about my recovery will certainly help. Thinking that things will only get worse will pull both me down and those around me trying to help.

It has been a great week for English cricket. Winning the first Test in Cardiff has put down a marker for the series. People were writing England off all winter, but the signs were there of a young talented team on the up. They have played good cricket all summer so far and I expect them to push the Aussies close.

15th July

IT'S A massive week for us in the T20. A win tonight and we should be close to qualifying and a second win on Friday would see us through.

It's been a tough last few days. Recovery has been slow and the symptoms in my legs are still occurring. Sam made a house visit to check up on me, he seemed happy with the way I was moving and was encouraged enough to let me go out for a walk twice a day. This may not seem like much, but to me it was like conquering Everest! I need to make sure that I don't get ahead of myself though as I'm not even two weeks out of surgery.

Notts are in a similar position to us in T20. They need to win both games to qualify for the quarter-finals. I arrived late to the game-Rooster had asked to see me for a check-up-so I pottered around the changing room trying to get the best seat. I thought our 137 was probably a few under par but the Notts bowlers executed their skills well and made scoring tough. We are very good at defending totals that we have no right to defend. We squeeze opponents in the middle overs not giving them an escape, and we did this with great affect here. Unfortunately James Taylor played a great knock to just get them over the line off the last ball to keep their quarter-final hopes alive. We now have two games left against the top two teams, Birmingham and Worcester, both away and have to win them to have any hope of qualifying.

I watched the final overs at home on television. Rooster had tapped me on the shoulder and gave me a stern reminder that I needed to be resting and that I had been doing too much. He was right. My leg was aching. I just wanted to be around though; I love the changing room. I needed that reminder to snap me out of it and remind me of the journey that lies ahead!

NatWest T20 Blast
Game 12 at Emirates Old Trafford, 15 July

Lancashire Lightning 137-4 (20 overs,
Brown 51, Croft 51, Faulkner 32*)
Notts Outlaws 140-7 (20 overs, Taylor 33*,
Hales 30, Clark 2-15)

Notts Outlaws won by 3 wickets

This was a low-scoring affair by T20 standards, with batsmen on both sides struggling throughout. Lancashire made a poor start, losing three wickets inside the first three overs, although Karl Brown continued his good form with 51 from 43 balls, and his innings was chiefly responsible for the Lightning reaching the halfway point on 57-3 with Brown having hit all of his side's eight boundaries at that point. Steven Croft hit the first six of the night off Samit Patel in the 11th over but immediately lost his partner when Brown hit Steven Mullaney hard and high to Rikki Wessels to make the Red Rose 70-4, ending a 57-run alliance. Croft, with 51 not out off 46, and James Faulkner (32 not out from 25) battled to get Lancashire up to some sort of defendable total, adding 67 over the remaining 50 balls, with only four further boundaries an indicator of the tough batting conditions, although Faulkner did wallop Jake Ball over mid-wicket for 6 in the 19th over.

If Lancashire's 137-4 looked below par at the interval, the Red Rose bowlers set about defending it in fine style. Kyle Jarvis bowled Michael Lumb for 11 in the 3rd over. The normally exuberant Alex Hales was contained to 30 off 28 balls before he drove Stephen Parry to Paul Horton at mid-on to make the Outlaws 80-3 in the 13th over, Wessels having cut Jordan Clark to Croft at backward point two overs earlier. The same Croft-Clark combination ended Patel's brief innings, 82-4, at the start of the 14th over but James Taylor held the Outlaws innings together, making an unbeaten 33 off 21 balls in a frantic finish. With 21 runs required from the last two overs it seemed that Lancashire might prevail, but Taylor hit the final two balls of the match for four as the visitors scored the 13 runs required from the final over to keep their T20 qualification hopes alive. The defeat left Lancashire precariously placed in fourth place with two games to go.

16th July

FOLLOWING THE telling off I received yesterday, and the signs of tiredness coming from my body, I lay back to watch the 2nd Test at Lord's. The painful feelings radiating from my leg were strong today. They are difficult to describe; an almost burning, prickly, sensation that comes and goes followed by sharp pains. The frustration has hit me today too as the realisation that this recovery won't be quick. It's going to test me mentally and physically.

17th July

YET ANOTHER boring day! The concept of doing nothing is setting in now, and it is not a good feeling. I'm naturally quite active and like being up and about. So I'm trying to find ways to make use of my time. I will have to have a career after cricket but what that is yet, I'm still unsure. The hardest part is choosing something to do. It's a scary thought to not think about cricket but something we, as cricketers, have to come to terms with. As you get older your motivations may change. I want to play cricket-I always have and always will. Looking to the future though, I have to start planning. How I am going to provide for my family and give them the best opportunity in life. Each day my leg seems to be getting better, although with the nerve growth rate of 1mm per day it could be some time before a full recovery is made.

The pitch at Lord's looks pretty flat! These conditions will suit the Aussies more than us. The flat pitch will nullify our bowlers and help their batters. I can't imagine they will have asked for a pitch like this. Hopefully we can get close to their monster score and get a draw out of the game. The 3rd Test is Edgbaston something of a stronghold for England. If we can go there 1-0 up the confidence will grow.

NatWest T20 Blast
Game 13 at Edgbaston, 17 July

Lancashire Lightning 145-6 (20 overs, Croft 64*)
Birmingham Bears 137 all out (19.5 overs,
McCullum 41, Faulkner 3-19, Croft 2-16)

Lancashire Lightning won by 8 runs

Lancashire held their nerve in this must-win game to keep their T20 hopes alive, winning by 8 runs. The Lightning's 145-6 after losing the toss was built upon Steven Croft's third successive fifty, his 51-ball 64 not out helping a recovery from 34-4 in the eighth over, and he shared 41 in 6.1 overs for the fifth wicket with Luke Procter, and 59 in 5.4 for the sixth with James Faulkner. Croft smashed his first six over mid-wicket in the 15th over off Oliver Hannon-Dalby, hit Ricky Gordon for successive boundaries and a six over square-leg in the 17th over, to take the Lightning beyond 100 and add 18 priceless runs, before reaching his fifty with a further six over square-leg off Hannon-Dalby in the 19th over. Faulkner joined in with a six of his own off the same bowler while two Croft boundaries in the last got Lancashire up to 145-6 with 52 runs arriving from the final four overs.

Brendon McCullum took the game to Lancashire with two sixes and two fours in the third over and successive sixes in the ninth, in an innings of 41 off 25 balls, but he was one of two wickets to fall to consecutive Croft deliveries in the tenth over as the Bears' slipped to 72-3 having lost Varun Chopra earlier to Kyle Jarvis for 8. Stephen Parry struck to get Clarke lbw in the 13th over, leaving the score at 86-4 and then, at the start of the 15th, Croft took stunning one-handed catch at short third-man above his head to help Faulkner get rid of Laurie Evans with 97 on the board. That left Birmingham needing 47 off 30 balls which had become 26 off 13 when Arron Lilley dismissed Tim Ambrose, caught at deep mid-wicket. Faulkner had Ateeq Javid and Gordon both caught from successive deliveries to leave the score at 123-8 with 22 required from 9 deliveries and Jordan Clark closed the game out with two wickets in the 20th over.

18th July

A TOUGH day, but good day. Lots of rest seems to have finally settled things down; the symptoms in my leg are easing and walking is getting a lot easier. Discipline is now a vital part of my bid to me regaining full fitness and I have to be careful now. An over-energetic day could set me back months.

It means that I'm still held up in my bed at the moment! Fortunately the amount of sport on television is helping, although the weather has halted play at The Open golf. The Test Match is still continuing and England are up against it! I wasn't too surprised at Clarke's decision not to enforce the follow-on though as there is still so much time left in the game. It won't hinder Australia's bid for the win with their aggressive batting order allowing the bowlers a well-earned rest, something they ably demonstrated by reaching the close on 108-0 off only 26 overs. England need a very good two days if they are to save this Test.

19th July

I'VE FELT a little drained today. I'm trying to keep myself positive because it's a beautiful day outside and all I want to do is play cricket. The Lanky lads have been really supportive of me while I've been side-lined. I'm gutted not to be out there playing alongside them, but they have been great with me. We have a great set of lads at the club who are all in it together win or lose.

They are at Colwyn Bay for a four-day game against Glamorgan. It's a home game for them but is closer to Manchester than their Cardiff HQ! It's a beautiful little ground too, and the atmosphere is always good due to the size of the ground while the wicket always seems to be batter-friendly. That was the case today with Browny carrying on his rich vein of form reaching another fifty. That proved to be the warm-up for Ashwell and Alviro. The class and experience shared between these two certainly showed today. Just listening to the radio commentary, it was clear that something special was happening. Once they get 'in' there is no stopping them. Alviro finished the day with an unbeaten double-century and to bat pretty much all day is tough, but to score 205 not out is taking it to another level. Princey finished on 154 not out to continue his monumental summer. He really seems to be enjoying himself at the moment, and it's showing in his batting. His inner drive to keep scoring runs is quite incredible.

It was a tough day for England though, losing the Test. The immediate, negative, reaction is quite unfair in my opinion. What people don't feel is the mental fatigue that accompanies spending that much time in the field while the opposition pile on the runs. It gets you down. Once England lost a couple of early wickets, that effect snowballed things to a rapid conclusion. Australia seem to have bounced back well from the opening defeat. Hopefully England will do so from this one.

20th July

A VERY wet day in Manchester! Being housebound it's always nice to get some visitors. Kyle Hogg and Phil Scott, our former strength and conditioning coach, came round for a brew to keep me company. It was actually a meeting of the bad backs!!

Hoggy had to retire last year due to a bad back, and Scotty had the same operation I had a few years ago. He has made a full recovery and is now England's S&C coach. This is massively encouraging for me to see someone who has made such a good recovery. Phil offered a few pearls of wisdom, and told me that, most of all, to take your time recovering. He came back a too bit early from his operation, causing himself complications later on. He was adamant that I rest and do nothing. My daily allowance of 200 yards to the top of the road and back was more than enough, he felt. He was also adamant that a strong mental attitude was vital for recovery.

The more I think about the mental side of things, it dawns on me that it affects everything. This is starting to show in the game at Colwyn Bay. Alviro and Ashwell have put together a 501-run stand! Five hundred runs! The mental energy and concentration required, along with the physical effort, is staggering. Both of them achieving career-best scores is very special and I wish I could have been there to watch it unfold.

Amassing a score of 698 for 5 declared doesn't happen every week. To the outside world the pitch must have seemed a batter's paradise, yet we had Glamorgan struggling on 165 for 6 by the end of the day. This is what spending nearly 140 overs in the field can do to a team. It drains you mentally, the opposition are on top, and you just can't fightback. Scoreboard pressure really does exist. For me, there's the added frustration that comes from missing these special moments. We spoke at the start of the season about enjoying each other's success. I can't wait to see both of them and congratulate them on their achievements. I would rather have been there, watching it live.

21st July

A DAY with no sport-well at least not on the TV! The second Test has been wrapped up and The Open championship done and dusted. Once again I'm struggling finding things to do. I can't leave the house; well I can go 200 yards! On days like this I feel life is passing me by-the new season can't come quickly enough. The future is playing on my mind a lot at the moment; a lot of 'what ifs'.

22nd July

BOREDOM!!! A couple of days into doing nothing and I'm totally bored. I know I have to rest to allow my back to heal, but the cabin fever is at an all-time high at the moment. I've tried to use mediation to help me relax and provide an escape, and even that isn't working. My back is starting to feel stronger which doesn't help the situation. I feel like I could do so much more, but one movement too much could cripple me again.

I'm missing the game a lot at the moment. Being out for this long does help you put the game in to perspective. I used to worry a lot about the little things; the 'ifs' and 'buts' and the fear of failure. This injury shows what can be just around the corner. Have I played my last game? Cricket is a game we enjoyed playing while growing up and we should never forget that.

I was cheered up when we managed to win the game at Colwyn Bay swiftly after lunch. Chappy edged ever closer to 1,000 wickets in his career, a feat that in my opinion will never be achieved again if Glen gets there. The win is a massive result too as it puts us well clear of Glamorgan who stay in third place and it means we are on the cusp of promotion. There is no better feeling than slugging it out for four days and coming out on top. A hard fought four-day win is the most satisfying for me. You know how hard you've had to work for every run and wicket to get the result.

LV= County Championship
Game 12 at Colwyn Bay, 19-22 July

Lancashire 698-5 dec
(Petersen 286*, Prince 261*, Brown 54)
Glamorgan 348 (Hogan 57, Chapple 4-62)
& (following-on) 193
(Cooke 56, Kerrigan 4-28, Lilley 3-38)

Lancashire won by an innings & 157 runs

Alviro Petersen and Ashwell Prince wrote their names into the record books, while Lancashire made a significant stride in their quest for promotion with a momentous victory by an innings and 157 runs against Glamorgan at Colwyn Bay.

Petersen hit a career-best 286 and Prince a career-best 261, the first time that two Lancashire players have scored a double hundred in the same innings, as the pair added a mammoth 501 runs for the third wicket to record Lancashire's highest-ever partnership for any wicket. It was also the fourth highest third-wicket partnership ever in first-class cricket and the second best third-wicket stand in the history of the County Championship, as well as being the 13th highest partnership for any wicket anywhere in the world. Petersen and Prince started their alliance just before 2pm on day one and were parted 89 overs later midway through the second day, allowing Steven Croft to declare before tea with the Red Rose on the huge score of 698-5.

A demoralised Glamorgan then reached 165-6 from 52 overs at close, with three of the wickets going to Glen Chapple with the new ball, before recovering to post a first-innings total of 348 thanks to last man Michael Hogan's 57 and solid batting by the tail. Chapple finished with an excellent 4-62.

Following-on, the home side struggled in their second innings as Lancashire's bowlers rammed home their advantage during the third afternoon and evening. Chris Cooke provided the main resistance with 56 but seven wickets between spinners Simon Kerrigan (4-28) and Arron Lilley (3-38) saw the Red Rose clinch victory early on the final day. The win gave Lancashire a huge 68-point advantage over third-placed Glamorgan with only four games left to play, although there now followed a gap of one month before their next Championship game.

23rd July

THE DAYS are flying by at the moment each day merging into the next. The thought of being able to drive next week is really motivating me; it means I will regain a sense of freedom. My 200-yard world will all of a sudden become a lot bigger!

I have to give credit to my wife Holly. She has been amazing throughout all this. I really haven't been able, or allowed, to do a thing. Even Sam reiterated this when he came round. I do feel guilty not helping, but realise I have to be a little selfish. I'm sure she will make me pay for it when I'm better!

The Women's Ashes games have been on the television over the last few days. It's great to see them doing well, inspiring thousands of young girls across the country. Kate Cross is doing a great job representing Lancashire as well.

Leicestershire's Matt Boyce retired from the game today. It's always sad to see someone leave the game, but he seems to have a career path in place for his future and feels that now is the right time to move on. A tough decision I'm sure, but I wish him all the best in his next chapter.

24th July

"IF YOU look too far forward, you may miss your first step." I love this quote and it's very appropriate for me at the moment. I'm starting to look so far down the line that I'm not concentrating on the present. My main focus is getting my back stronger. The symptoms seem to be fading away, although it's still in spasm on the right side causing a shift. Until this shift resolves I can't really progress much on my rehab programme. My daily exercises are helping, but the pace at which I can see improvement is slow. Highly frustrating.

Great to see the lads qualify for the T20 quarter-finals today. Even though it was due to a washout, I feel we deserved the spot. Rain across the whole country meant no-one could play; we qualified due to a superior run-rate over Notts. Things seem to be falling our way this year. If we can keep hold of Jimmy (Anderson) and have Jos (Buttler) available, then I can genuinely see us winning the trophy.

NatWest T20 Blast
Game 14 at Worcester, 24 July

Worcs Rapids v Lancashire Lightning

Match abandoned due to rain

Lancashire Lightning's bid to win their first t20 title remained alive after rain washed out both their game at Worcester and, crucially, Notts' game at Leicester. The 'no-results' meant that Lancashire, level on points with Notts going into the final round of games, stayed in fourth place by having a superior net-run rate and qualified for the quarter-finals.

25th July

I WILL remember this day for the rest of my life. Holly found out she is pregnant.

All my worries about my back have vanished. In five minutes my whole world has changed, and new responsibilities and demands will be expected of me.

Getting fit seems to have taken on a new meaning. I'm doing it for my family now. I guess our lives will change now as certain things will become less important and others more so.

Growing up, I was fortunate enough that my parents gave me the best chance at succeeding in cricket. If it wasn't for them, then I wouldn't be in the position I am today. I want to do that for my children.

I don't want to get too far ahead of myself. If I don't get my back right all that I have mentioned above will mean nothing.

26th July

AFTER THE elation of yesterday, the rain has brought a damper feel to today. The lads are on a southern tour starting with Sussex today. Looking at the weather forecast, play looks highly doubtful. Rain delays can be very frustrating and players tend to find different things to do to pass the time. Some listen to music, some play cards, while others read the paper or are immersed in some form of learning. If the facilities are available, it's also a good chance to top up on your skills indoors.

Back at Old Trafford, the new 50-over kit is being revealed today. The phrase 'Lancashire Limes' may get used a few times! It's a lime green colour combo that matches the sponsor's logo colour. I think it doesn't look too bad, but I'm sure there will be some contrasting opinions!

After a catch up with Sam and Rooster, I've been allowed to walk for a little longer. Four separate spells of five minutes per day. This may not seem a lot but, at the moment, to me it's like running a marathon!

Royal London One-Day Cup
Game 1 at Horsham, 26 July

Sussex v Lancashire

Match abandoned due to rain

27th July

IN SPORT you are lucky to have access to a number of different outlets to help in different areas. I had a great chat with Lee Richardson, the club's sports psychologist today. Lee comes from a sporting background, after playing and managing in professional football, and really understands our situations. Being able to air my frustrations to him over the last few months has certainly helped me to relax and feel at ease with the situation.

Together we tried to form some sort of plan for the next stage of my career; retirement. I still hope to play a lot more cricket, but it's good to plan for the future and this also gives me something to channel my energy into at the moment.

We had a great chat mapping out the next few years and putting in some markers that will show progression and movement forward. I felt a lot more comfortable with the idea after doing this. It's a scary thing to think of life without cricket, but the more prepared you are for it the better it will be.

After yesterday's washout the lads travelled to Essex for another 50-over game today. Essex are normally a strong one day team who have a good record in white ball cricket. It would be great to get a win here to get a foothold in our group. Hopefully the weather isn't the same as it is here. It's only good for ducks!

28th July

A DISAPPOINTING loss for us last night. Being put in to bat with a 10.30 am start can be tricky, especially after all the wet weather we have had recently. I chatted to a few of the lads after the game who said the pitch wasn't the best and favoured the bowlers early on. Sometimes, through luck more than anything, you can get through those early stages without losing wickets. Unfortunately we kept losing them at regular stages, allowing no momentum to build. Defending a score of 161 was never going to be easy and the only way to win was to bowl them out. Ravi Bopara played well by the sound of it; taking four wickets and then making an unbeaten century to win the game meant he'd had a pretty good day. Losing certainly makes the bus journey longer on the way home!

We need to bounce back straight away at Blackpool tomorrow to make sure we don't fall too far behind in this competition. Blackpool is a lovely ground and, as with most outgrounds, it has a very intimate feel with the crowd right on top of you. The last time I played there, a water balloon was catapulted from over the wall in Stanley Park and landed right on a length. It couldn't have been aimed any better! Fortunately it didn't affect the pitch too much.

Royal London One-Day Cup
Game 2 at Chelmsford, 27 July

Lancashire 161-9 (50 overs, Davies 37, Bopara 4-31)
Essex 163-3 (33 overs, Bopara 101*)

Essex won by 7 wickets

Ravi Bopara excelled with ball and bat as Lancashire slipped to a Royal London Cup defeat to Essex at Chelmsford.

The Red Rose batsmen found the going tough in favourable bowling conditions, with swing and seam movement prevalent, and they struggled to a disappointing 161-9 from their 50 overs with Bopara taking four wickets while Reece Topley struck twice and David Masters returned an excellent 1-20 from his ten overs. Karl Brown and Alviro Petersen added 40 for the second wicket and Alex Davies top-scored with 37, sharing 44 for the sixth with Jordan Clark but Lancashire, 44-1 in the 15th over then lost five wickets for 22 runs in nine overs, and the innings never really recovered.

Bopara then eased his way to a century with 101 not out off 98 balls, ably supported by Mark Pettini who hit 37 and their partnership of 98 inside 20 overs took Essex to a comfortable seven-wicket victory with 17 overs still remaining.

29th July

GAME DAY at Blackpool and it's sunny for once which makes a pleasant change from the last few days. It will be a hard game as Middlesex are an organised team with a lot of experience in their ranks. It's not been the best of starts to the group stage for us, and while the aim is to win the group if possible, all you have to do to reach the knock-out stages is finish in fourth place, so we are still in with a good chance.

Not playing is really starting to get to me, especially on days like this. Watching cricket is fun, but nothing beats playing. There is no better feeling than walking out there representing Lancashire. It is special every time you get the opportunity to do so. As tough as it is at the moment, I know that if I keep to the programme, then I will be back out there wearing the Red Rose in the future.

The third Ashes Test starts today, and for me it couldn't have come quick enough. Jeremy Kyle wasn't quite cutting it for daytime viewing! There has been a lot of talk about the team and players moving up/down the order. Unfortunately for Gary Ballance he has missed out, with Ian Bell moving up to three. Tough on Ballance as his Test career to date has been solid. It shows the cutthroat nature of professional sport, but I'm sure he will come back stronger from it.

On the injury front there's not too much to report, which is good. The tingling sensations in my legs are slowly easing, allowing for freer movement.

Royal London One-Day Cup
Game 3 at Blackpool, 29 July

Middlesex 161 all out (46.5 overs,
Harris 32, Bailey 3-31)
Lancashire 162-8 (48 overs,
Brown 36, Faulkner 35, Junaid 3-32)

Lancashire won by 2 wickets

A terrific bowling performance plus a match-winning partnership of 47 between James Faulkner and Jordan Clark took Lancashire through to a nervy two-wicket win against Middlesex in a low-scoring thriller at Blackpool.

On a sun drenched, albeit windy, day at the seaside the Red Rose seam bowlers prospered, reducing the Seaxes to 83-7 after 27 overs with Tom Bailey claiming a one-day best 3-31 from eight overs. None of the Middlesex top order looked particularly comfortable in the bowler-friendly conditions, and it took two late order partnerships of 28 between John Simpson (20) and James Harris (32), and 50 between Harris and Toby Roland-Jones (29), to help the visitors struggle to 161 all out from 46.5 overs.

Karl Brown hit a rapid 38 to steer Lancashire to 59-2 but the home side lost regular wickets to reach the halfway stage of their innings in trouble on 93-6. Faulkner and Clark slowly chipped away to bring the required target down, although the pair had an almighty let-off with the scoreboard reading 102-6, when Middlesex fluffed a run-out chance with both batsmen at the same end. With 60 runs still required it was a pivotal moment, and the Red Rose pair made the most of their let-off to slowly advance the score to 140 before Faulkner on 35 (from a patient 82 deliveries) could do little to get out of the way of a lifter from Junaid Khan that the Australian gloved to slip. When Clark departed for 22, the outcome was still uncertain with 15 runs required and two wickets left. To take advantage of the conditions, Middlesex had stuck largely with their four front-line seam bowlers and all had bowled their 10-over allocation by the end of the 45th over. It was an understandable gamble, but Stephen Parry and Bailey batted out the last overs by James Franklin and Harris and then picked off the runs required from the spinners to seal victory with two overs left.

30th July

OFF AND running! It was great for the lads to get over the line yesterday with a win. A close one at that, but a win is a win! Getting into the habit of winning the tight ones is huge. It builds confidence that you can perform as a team and as an individual in high-pressure situations. This was the case in 2011 (when we won the County Championship) and in last year's T20 run when we reached the final; we got over the line in tight games and never looked back. This could be our kickboard to a Lord's final! I have been constantly texting the physio all day asking for updates; I was nervous just listening to the radio commentary!

Not being able to affect the game is the worst feeling ever. If you are playing you can do something to help, but otherwise you are just helpless. Momentum in sport is massive. Look at the Ashes; neither team have managed to get the upper hand. England after their win at Cardiff, and then the Aussies after their victory at Lord's. The 3rd Test always shapes the series, and I feel that whoever comes out on top at Edgbaston will go on to win it. If England have a good day today, the Ashes could be theirs. I sense there is a growing belief throughout the country that it could happen.

31st July

ANOTHER MONTH gone! I had a good catch up with Rooster and Sam about my back and its movement in the near future. Things are going well, although the tasks I have to perform are very simple and very mundane. Rooster described the first six weeks as the danger zone, which means another two weeks of literally doing nothing. No driving, lifting, twirling or spinning. Nothing.

I'm having good days and bad days at the moment. The frustration of not being able to do anything is certainly getting to me and I keep on having to remind myself that things could be a lot worse! On my bad days I use my meditation techniques to try and cope with the frustration and they certainly help.

The Test almost looked like it could be over inside two days! The Aussies are 23 ahead with three wickets left. If they can somehow get a 120-150 lead they may have a chance. Johnson and Starc would need to fire and England would need to bat horribly, but it is sport and anything is possible! Let's hope England can go 2-1 up!

AUGUST

Winning and grinning

Dancing the night away: joining in with our celebrations on the pitch at Edgbaston after winning the NatWest T20 Blast final

1st August

IT'S AUGUST already. It doesn't seem two minutes ago that I was walking out for the toss at Derby in the first game of the season. How things have changed. Once the season gets going, time flies. You go from one ground to another, forever travelling up and down the motorways. It's part of being a county cricketer and, as tough as the schedule can be at times, it's part of what we do. The friendships you make and the memories you have will be there forever, and are all forged on these journeys.

Not that I'm travelling far today! Not much is going on today in the world of sport either, other than the Rugby League Challenge Cup semi-finals are on TV. Give me 90mph deliveries any day over one of those boys running flat out at me!

I'm still getting occasional shooting pains in my leg, which does freak me out every now and then. Yesterday was probably the most frustrated I have been so far and keeping a positive mind is key here. The boredom really got to me though, I just wanted to get out there and play-even if it meant fielding all day!

2nd August

THE LADS are playing at Old Trafford today so I popped down to catch up with them all. It felt great to be out of the house but most of all to be back in the changing room with the lads. It really is an amazing place and part of the game that I will miss when my time is up. I've always found watching tough and it's even harder when I can't get out there and play. I try and help as much as I can when I'm there, while trying not to get in the way.

It was a tough defeat for the lads. It's never nice to lose, especially at home and in a close game. Saying that, just like the T20, if we can qualify after that it's knock-out cricket and anything can happen. Birmingham are a prime example; they finished fourth in the group stages of the T20 last year and went on to win it. You can fly under the radar, and no-one seems to notice you until you are lifting the trophy at the end.

It was a sad end to the one-day game on TV at Cardiff between Glamorgan and Hampshire. The game was abandoned due to a dangerous pitch and the delivery to Hampshire's Jimmy Adams was a nasty one. He was lucky to come out of it unharmed, but things could have been a lot different. I feel it was the correct decision, as the batters would not have been able to trust the pitch due to the fear of it happening again. With the events of the recent past following the death of Phil Hughes, the safety of the players comes first, so this was the correct decision. The game is hard enough without having to worry about the ball hitting you on the head off a length.

Royal London One-Day Cup
Game 4 at Emirates Old Trafford, 2 August

Lancashire 265-7 (50 overs,
Prince 82, Davies 73*, Rankin 3-33)
Warwickshire 268-7 (49.5 overs,
Chopra 88, Ambrose 59, Parry 2-30)

Warwickshire won by 3 wickets

Warwickshire won by three wickets with one ball to spare in a thrilling finish, to put a dent in Lancashire's Royal London Cup hopes.

It was a game that ebbed and flowed throughout with the result in doubt until Ateeq Javid carved the fifth ball of the final over to the third man boundary to clinch victory for the visitors.

Put in to bat, Lancashire overcame the early loss of the in-form Karl Brown for 7 with Ashwell Prince and Alviro Petersen combining to add 62 runs inside 12 overs for the second wicket. Paul Horton also made 37 in a 75-run partnership with Prince to put the Red Rose in a good position at 154-3 in the 31st over. Prince continued his outstanding batting this season with an innings of 82 from 87 balls which included five fours to go with his one six on a sluggish wicket that required patience from the batsmen. Alex Davies led the chase for runs over the closing fifteen overs with a quite marvellous, unbeaten, one-day best of 73 from 59 balls and shared a 79-run partnership for the 6th wicket with James Faulkner as Lancashire closed on a healthy 265-7.

Varun Chopra and Will Porterfield raced away at the start of the Bears reply, reaching the end of the 10-over powerplay on 60-0. Stephen Parry and Faulkner both struck with a wicket apiece, while Steven Croft and Parry combined to restrict the scoring as the visitors reached the halfway point on 116-2. Chopra reached his fifty from 75 balls and the Warwickshire skipper found great support from Tim Ambrose who struck a fine 59 in a century partnership before being trapped lbw by Kyle Jarvis to leave the Bears 173-3 in the 35th over. Rikki Clarke pulled the excellent Parry (2-30 from 10 overs) to Prince at long-on to depart for 5, and Croft struck twice to remove Laurie Evans for 11 and Chopra, bowled playing back, for 88 to make Lancashire slight favourites with the Bears 211-6 in the 44th over. Keith Barker and Ateeq Javid then added 27 runs from 22 balls before Barker departed, but Jeetan Patel and Javid (who finished 32 not out) hit further boundaries to leave 13 required off the final six deliveries. Patel hit a further four off the first ball of the last over before Javid, with six runs required from three, hit consecutive boundaries to steer the Bears home with one ball to spare.

3rd August

IT DAWNED on me this morning that there are only eight weeks left in the season. We are now down to the nitty gritty stage of things. The games carry more clout now as the end of the season nears and the prospect of winning a trophy becomes closer. These are the games you want to be playing in.

There has been some chatter about the constant switching of formats, especially in the early part of the season. To jump from championship cricket to T20 can be tough. The Friday night games are great and we have been well supported as per usual at Old Trafford. Finishing a Championship game on a Wednesday and then jumping straight into a T20 game on the Friday doesn't leave a great deal of time for preparation. If we are away, you can be traveling on the Thursday allowing little, if any, time for practice. Admittedly some players cope with this 'crossover' better than others. However, if we want to emulate the Aussies' Big Bash and the IPL then surely players need to be at their best, having honed their skills in the nets. It's a debate that needs sorting out soon.

It was four weeks today that I went under the knife and things seem to be progressing quite nicely. My leg feels a lot stronger but the time frame is still unclear. From the reading I have been doing it's clear that a positive mind and a focus on what I want will help me recover.

4th August

IT'S A game day for the lads, and they are at Liverpool for another one-day cup match. I've good memories from playing at Aigburth. We always have great support, the wicket is brilliant and always allows for an entertaining game of cricket, and on top of that the lunches are fantastic! We get chips, chicken nuggets, and there's usually some cheesecake. We love it but I'm sure our fitness coach isn't as happy.

Nottinghamshire seem to be playing some good cricket at the moment. Peter Moores has joined them recently and they seem to be on the rise. It wouldn't surprise me if he had something to do with it. He is a brilliant coach who is constantly trying to get the best out of you, always striving for improvement. His record speaks for itself and Notts are lucky to have him.

I'm off to the gym today and it may seem 'sad', but I can't wait. These small steps of progression really help to keep me going. I can then move to the next one, and so on, until before you know it you are back in the middle. There is always a little bit of apprehension before I start, but Dave Roberts and his team, notably Sam, have always looked after me well, no matter what the injury or concern I've had. Without them I wouldn't have played the majority of the cricket I have.

The session went well though. Dave and Sam put my leg and back through some mobilisation movements trying to wake up the nerves in my leg. At the start there was still some intense pain in my shin, but as we progressed it became more bearable and calmer. There is still a long way to go but it's a start.

5th August

WAKING UP this morning I was expecting to feel sore and stiff. Rooster did mention there could be some strange sensations after the work we did. It was a very pleasant surprise to wake up feeling fine. This was both a relief and a massive morale boost to know I could perform some basic functions without any problematic side-effects.

I felt for the lads after yesterday's game. It looked at one point that we might just nick it, but Chris Read, as he has done on many occasions, came in and showed the value of experience. He has been involved in a number of lower order partnerships that have been crucial for Notts and helped them win some games they probably shouldn't. Even so, I'm sure the lads are disappointed not to get over the line. We can still qualify, all is not lost yet, but I feel we will have to win the remaining games and hope some results go our way elsewhere.

Royal London One-Day Cup
Game 5 at Liverpool, 4 August

Lancashire 216-8 (50 overs, Brown 77, Patel 3-31) Nottinghamshire 217-6 (46.4 overs, Taylor 56, Read 47*, Griffiths 3-41)

Nottinghamshire won by 4 wickets

Notts Outlaws ran out four-wicket winners at Aigburth to leave Lancashire's Royal London Cup hopes hanging by a thread after a third defeat in the competition. A half century by visiting skipper James Taylor was followed by a match-winning 71-run partnership between Chris Read and Brett Hutton to steer the Outlaws home with 20 balls to spare.

Karl Brown was the mainstay of the Red Rose innings with 77, but only found support from Steven Croft who made 38. The pair added 66 for the fourth wicket as Lancashire reached the end of the second powerplay well-placed on 152-3 after 40 overs. The attempted acceleration over the final ten overs failed to materialise as five wickets fell for 42 runs in six overs, with the final total a below-par 216-8.

Undaunted the bowlers hit back, led by Gavin Griffiths who dismissed Rikki Wessels for 6, and then took an outstanding catch off his own bowling to account for Alex Hales for 32. Two balls later Griffiths was on his way to a career-best 3-41, celebrating the scalp of Brendon Taylor who drove to mid-off to put Notts in trouble on 53-3 in the 11th over. Samit Patel and James Taylor steadied the Outlaws reply with a 51-run partnership, but after three wickets fell to the spin of Stephen Parry and Arron Lilley, the visitors were 146-6 and still 71 runs away from their target. Read, with a trademark one-day innings of 47 from 45 balls and Hutton (33 off 41), refused to buckle and steered their side to victory with 20 balls remaining.

8th August

Royal London One-Day Cup
Game 6 at Canterbury, 8 August

Lancashire 258-9 (50 overs, Livingstone 91,
Davies 57, Croft 55, Coles 4-34)
Kent 207 all out (37.4 overs, Blake 89, Parry 3-60)

Lancashire won by 51 runs

Liam Livingstone's maiden first-team fifty, an 88-ball 91, and a slick bowling and fielding display helped to boost Lancashire's Royal London Cup quarter-final hopes by hammering Kent at Canterbury, and put down a marker ahead of the two sides' forthcoming T20 clash the following week.

Livingstone displayed power and finesse during his hour and a half at the crease and he led an impressive recovery from 26-3, adding 112 inside 22 overs with Steven Croft, who made 55, and 68 in eight overs with Alex Davies (57) for the fifth wicket, to advance the score to 206-5 after 40 overs. The innings stumbled slightly over the final ten, but Lancashire's 258-9 proved far too good for the hosts.

The Red Rose attack struck three times inside the first 18 overs of the run chase as the home side fell to 79-3, and when captain Sam Northeast and Fabian Cowdrey fell in successive balls in the 21st over, the latter to a run out by Alviro Petersen, Kent were in a spot of bother at 87-5. Despite a late assault from Alex Blake, who hit 89 off 56 balls including seven sixes, wickets continued to tumble with Stephen Parry taking 3-60 while Jordan Clark and James Faulkner claimed two each. Faulkner finished proceedings when he bowled Blake with more than 12 overs remaining.

15th August

NatWest T20 Blast
Quarter-Final at Canterbury, 15 August

Kent 142 all out (20 overs, Tredwell 31*, Parry 3-31)
Lancashire 142-6 (20 overs,
Prince 62, Buttler 53, Coles 3-22)

Scores level - Lancashire won by having
lost fewer wickets

Lancashire made it to Finals Day for the second year in a row after a dramatic, last-ball victory over Kent Spitfires at Canterbury.

After Steven Croft won the toss, two wickets for Kyle Jarvis with successive deliveries in the fifth over saw Kent slip to 25-2. Arron Lilley struck with his first ball in the ninth over with just 53 on the board to get Sam Northeast, the competition's leading run-scorer lbw for only 14. That was the first of three wickets to fall in 14 balls, with Lilley next involved in an astonishing catch. Darren Stevens lofted a Stephen Parry delivery high towards the boundary, but could only watch as Lilley ran from deep mid-wicket to deep square before palming what looked to be a certain six back into the field of play, where Karl Brown completed the catch. Lilley then trapped Alex Blake lbw for 2 and despite 27 from Sam Billings, the home side were in deep trouble after two Parry wickets left them on 86-7 in the 14th. A partnership of 52 off 34 balls by Fabian Cowdrey (27) and James Tredwell (31 not out off 14) revived Spitfire hopes as the home side finished on 142 all out, with James Faulkner taking two wickets with the last two balls of the innings.

Ashwell Prince expertly anchored the Lancashire innings, which had reached 50-2 in the 8th over when Liam Livingstone pulled Tredwell for six, before falling lbw to the Kent spinner for 12. Jos Buttler hit his fourth ball over long-on for six as the Lightning reached halfway at 64-3. Prince reached his 40-ball fifty in the 13th over as Lancashire closed in on their target, passing 100 in the 15th over. When Buttler hit his third six straight off Tredwell in the 16th over to bring up the pair's 50 partnership, and followed with three fours from the last four balls of the 18th over against Ivan Thomas, the game looked to be well in Lancashire's grasp with 13 runs required off two overs. Prince fell for 62 to the first ball of the 19th over but crucially Buttler reverse-paddled the final ball of the over for four to reach a 36-ball fifty, which left six runs needed from the last over from Matt Coles.

Steven Croft pushed a single, then Buttler on 53 departed to a catch by Blake at long-on before Croft fell to a catch by Cowdrey from the following ball. Faulkner swung at, but missed, his first delivery which meant, incredibly, five runs were now required from the last two balls. Faulkner got two runs down to long-on, and with Lilley running hard at the non-striker's end, scrambled two to long-on from the final ball to tie the game and seal the win on fewer wickets lost. It was a heart-stopping finale in a match which, until that last over, never looked like finishing so dramatically.

16th August

IT'S AN early start today to meet Rooster at the gym in Chorley. My progress has been good so far. I've upped my walking to 12 minutes at a time, three times a day. My hamstring stretch is getting back to normal and the strength in my shin is slowly showing signs of recovery. As boring a recovery as this is, the signs are pointing in the right direction. The trouble is I have to remain doing very little.

Today was a momentous day, I was able to do one length of front crawl. I was knackered at the end of it, blowing! My first proper exercise for nearly two months. It felt very odd at first; my arms almost forgot what they were meant to do. It doesn't sound like much, but it was a great breakthrough session and driving home I felt great. Things are slowly on the mend and the weeks of doing nothing were finally starting to show some reward.

While on my journey home I found out about Liam Livingstone and what had happened to him. (Note: Liam was the victim of an unprovoked attack in a bar and hit in the face with a glass while celebrating with the Lancashire team following the T20 win at Canterbury.) A truly cowardly act of aggression. To inflict that kind of injury upon another human being seems unthinkable. We can only hope he is okay.

I'm sure all the lads are shaken up by the incident. It is truly horrific what has happened.

17th August

GOOD NEWS. Thankfully 'Livi' seems to have escaped without any serious damage to his eye. The pictures I've seen show a story of a grotesque assault. Fingers crossed he will be okay for T20 Finals Day.

The news that James Faulkner will also be available for Finals Day is a massive boost. He has shown his qualities on a number of occasions this summer and will be a huge asset.

For me it was back to the pool. After the success of yesterday Rooster was keen to see me try and repeat the session, and afterwards my leg showed no signs of inflammation and was pain free. The symptoms have now pretty much faded away. I get the odd pulse down my leg but nothing like it was before the operation. Rooster is keen to hammer home the importance of keeping up with my exercises and not rushing into anything yet. I feel really good at the moment, although the frustration of not being able to do anything is getting to me.

After the T20 exploits of Saturday-and the drama of Sunday-the lads had to get back to the 50-over competition today. Yet again Ashwell showed all his experience in compiling a match-winning hundred, ably supported by Alviro. The partnership between these two is strong. Setting 301 for victory was a great achievement and provided instant scoreboard pressure. Despite the valiant efforts of Adam Wheater with 111, Hampshire fell 30 runs short of their target. This game had a lot of significance; it kept us in the hunt for a quarter-final spot and to get one over them before the T20 semi-final was massive. With the cricket we are playing at the moment it wouldn't surprise me if we ended up with the treble.

Royal London One-Day Cup
Game 7 at Southampton, 17 August

Lancashire 301-4 (50 overs, Prince 102, Petersen 82)
Hampshire 272 all out (49.1 overs,
Wheater 111, Adams 53, Dawson 52, Jarvis 3-46)

Lancashire won by 29 runs

A century by Ashwell Prince helped Lancashire keep their quarter-final hopes alive in the Royal London Cup with a 29-run win.

Prince hit 102 off 113 balls, equalling his best one-day score in a Red Rose shirt, to lead the Lightning to an excellent score of 301-4, and the left-hander shared a Lancashire one-day record 147 runs in 24 overs for the second wicket against Hampshire with compatriot Alviro Petersen, who also impressed with 82 off 84 balls. Earlier Prince and Karl Brown, who made 40, laid the foundations with an opening partnership of 73 in 16 overs, while Steven Croft, James Faulkner and Alex Davies helped add 80 runs over the final 10 overs.

Adam Wheater's 111 from 114 balls kept Hampshire in the hunt, and following a century partnership with Chris Adams, the home side reached the 30-over mark in decent shape on 160-3. But Wheater kept losing partners at key moments as the Lancashire attack built up the pressure. Needing 82 from the final 10 overs, Stephen Parry ended Wheater's innings in the 42nd over and facing a mounting run-rate, wickets tumbled as Hampshire were bowled out for 272 from the first ball of the final over.

18th August

FRUSTRATION!

The quote I made early in the diary "if you look too far forward, you will miss your first step" is ringing true today.

The frustration of not being able to play, coupled with my doubts for the future exploded today. It's been one of those days that you're best off just forgetting. I'm so eager to get started on the future that I'm forgetting what is happening now. A lot of my energy needs be focused on getting fit and continuing my career. The temptation to look too far ahead will only distract me from that. Working out what you want to do is tough especially when you are living your dream. Holly bore the brunt of this little wobble; she managed to calm me making me refocus on what was important.

The forecast doesn't look too good for tomorrow's crucial game. We need to win and hope that Kent vs. Middlesex gets called off. The way it's looking both games may be abandoned.

19th August

THE WEATHER ruled unfortunately. The forecast hasn't looked too good for a few days and needing a win to qualify, the rain is the last thing we need. The pitch looked good to be fair and that showed with the way Ashwell and Browny played.

For me, excitement was building. My follow-up appointment is scheduled for tomorrow and things seem to be okay. The pool sessions are tedious but they are getting the job done. My back shift seems to be resolving slowly and the strength in my shin is returning.

Also the final Ashes Test starts and that will kill some of the boredom. Hopefully England can press on and finish the series in style.

Royal London One-Day Cup
Game 8 at Emirates Old Trafford, 19 August

Lancashire 68-0 (8.4 overs, Prince 38*, Brown 29*)
Glamorgan did not bat

Match abandoned due to rain - No Result

Requiring a win to have any chance of qualifying, the final group game at Old Trafford was washed away by rain with less than nine overs played to end Lancashire's interest in the Royal London Cup.

20th August

IT WAS a very mixed day today. The last few weeks I have been up and down mood-wise. Today was my follow-up meeting with Mr Leggate. My leg has been good for a number of days now; some flickers here and there, but generally things are looking positive. The meeting couldn't have gone better. He asked some basic questions about my general state and then performed a few tests. I still have some work to do regaining the strength and power in my shin. That was to be expected, but overall he was very happy and expects me to make a full recovery.

The last time I walked out of his office I was nearly in tears, this time I was grinning from ear to ear!

This news has given me a massive confidence boost for my up and coming rehab phase. It will be slow and tedious but I will get better.

On the flip side of this, my good friend Paul Horton was released by Lancashire today. It's always sad when someone leaves the club especially after such a long time. It's something that will happen to us all at some point and, as much as you anticipate it, probably nothing could prepare you for that news. He certainly has a lot to offer to anyone, and I'm sure he will do well wherever he goes.

21st August

AFTER THE good news of yesterday rehab today didn't seem too tedious. My regular morning pool session seemed to fly by, thanks to my new extra positive outlook.

Sam has introduced a few more new exercises into my programme today. I still have a slight shift which needs to be resolved. My body is so used to being in a position that protects my back, it has now become the norm! I have to trust now that it won't hurt and also correct that fear in my mind.

As sad as the news was yesterday of Paul leaving the club, it does present an opportunity for someone and Haseeb Hameed has impressed at a lot of levels. It's a special time when someone makes their debut for the club. I still remember starting out on my career at Lancashire many years ago now. Hopefully he will have a successful career ahead of him.

The weather dominated a lot of today and with Surrey looking on top in their game we need to try and get a result or they could overtake us in the run-in. With the forecast as it is, we may struggle. The weather was a lot better down south for the Test Match. Australia have enjoyed a good couple of days and are well on top. It is great to see Peter Siddle getting a game; by the looks of things it's maybe one game too late. I think he would have been quite handy at Trent Bridge! This series has been up and down throughout. The mental exhaustion of the England players may be showing in this fixture. All the energy they've put into the last few games to win the Ashes may have taken its toll. I'm sure they will want to finish on a high though!

22nd August

AFTER THE confidence boost I've received from seeing the specialist, rehab has become a lot less tedious! Now that I feel more confident, I'm trying to move forward quicker than I actually can and Rooster and Sam have to keep reminding me that it's a marathon not a sprint.

I managed to get down to Old Trafford just in time to see Karl Brown make his century. It's been coming over the last few games, and with the form he's been in it's not surprising. The lads were well chuffed for him, as we are when anyone does well. There was a funny story to go with it too. Browny was 80 not out overnight and this morning was greeted by Stan, the steward on the player's entrance, with the immortal advice, "don't cock it up today Karl"!

The game itself is moving forward. The rain isn't helping us push for victory, which is annoying as Surrey seem to be consolidating a strong position at Gloucester. If they manage to get a win and we don't, they will go top. Yes, we want to get promotion, but we want to win the division.

At the Oval an Australian victory in the Test is looming. I'm sure the England boys will be gutted to lose, but the series has been won and the urn is staying here. It must be an incredible feeling.

23rd August

SUNDAYS TEND to be pretty relaxing in my rehab. Rest is just as important as it allows the body to adapt to all the work you have been doing. I was asked to speak at the club's Foundation Dinner, something that I jumped at the chance to do. Our Foundation does a lot of work in the community helping people less fortunate than others.

I caught a little bit of the cricket, and our bowlers worked hard on a pretty flat wicket to get six wickets. Unfortunately the weather halted play and brought an early close. I couldn't have timed my walk to the car any worse. In 50 yards I managed to get soaking wet, but it was a sign how far I've come that all that went through my mind was that "worse things can happen."

24th August

I MET Rooster bright and early at the David Lloyd gym in Manchester for my regular pool session. Sometimes these sessions just drag, and today was one of those. Thirty minutes in the pool felt like an eternity and boring. Times like this make you question what you are doing, and I suppose I needed a kick up the backside. Rooster is the perfect man for this job. He snapped me out of the zombie-like state I was in, reminding me that if I don't do things right now, my rehab will be longer. That did it. I quickly refocused on what I had to do! Boring, yes, but essential to my future.

LV= County Championship
Game 13 at Emirates Old Trafford, 21-24 August

Lancashire 462 (Brown 132, Davies 95,
Croft 67, Faulkner 63, Meschede 4-101)
Glamorgan 213 (Kerrigan 4-60)
& following-on 159-3 (Rudolph 63)

Match Drawn

It might have been one month (and ten one-day games) since Lancashire's previous Championship match, but the Red Rose side made a good start against third-placed Glamorgan finishing a truncated first day on 161-3. Karl Brown continued his great form in making an unbeaten 80, while 18-year-old Haseeb Hameed was handed his first-class debut and made a composed 28. Brown went on to score the second first-class century of his career on day two making a fine 132 and sharing a 132-run partnership with Steven Croft who made 67. Some quick scoring by Alex Davies steered Lancashire to 300-4 with two balls of the 110th over remaining and the wicketkeeper/batsman went on to make a hard-hitting 95, adding 128 runs inside 23 overs with James Faulkner who struck 63 from 70 balls as Lancashire finished 462 all out.

Glamorgan lost an early wicket before the close and five more in the 52 overs and two balls possible on day three, to leave the visitors on 182-6 with rain again curtailing play early. When Simon Kerrigan took three early wickets to help bowl the visitors out for 213 in 40 minutes on the final morning and force the follow-on, the Red Rose were in with an outside chance of victory. A resolute batting display, on an increasingly slow pitch, saw the visitors through to the close on 159-3 in their second innings, and the teams shook hands on the draw at 5.20pm with nine overs remaining. The result left Lancashire just five points away from clinching promotion.

25th August

FOLLOWING A good, progressive session yesterday today was more about relaxing. A walk in the morning, then another at midday and in the evening was the sum of my day along with my exercises. With the confidence in my leg increasing, I need to make sure I rest so I can work to the best of my ability when I need to. Meanwhile, morning sickness is taking over Hol at the moment, so tending to her is becoming more like being a waiter than a husband. It's weird to think she's growing an actual human inside her body!

26th August

WITH THE weekend approaching the thought of T20 Finals Day gets more and more exciting. It's a special day to play in and I'm sure it will be even better this time when we win, I'm that confident.

The buzz amongst the group is growing. Having played in a couple of Finals Days now it's safe to say, as a county player, it doesn't get much better. The atmosphere is electric all day, largely fuelled I suspect by the alcohol consumed throughout! I can also feel the frustration growing at missing out. The big games are the ones you want to play in; they excite you and are the times you remember. However I have ultimate faith in the process I am going through, and that it will lead me back on to the cricket field. Along the way though, I have been tested and I'm sure I will be again.

Training was intense as the boys had a middle practice, although there was some sad news that Kyle Jarvis had broken a bone in his hand, ending his season. Kyle has had a golden summer, and has been a key player in all formats. You could see the look in his eye, he was gutted. I took him to one side consoling him, explaining that it wasn't all bad, that he could be proud of what he has accomplished this year. He's a great lad Jarv, and he will certainly come back stronger.

27th August

TIME SEEMS to be standing still at the moment. Finals Day is just around the corner, but the clocks don't seem to be moving quickly enough! You can tell the boys just want to play, the energy is building and all the talk is about winning. Nothing else is even thought about and confidence is high. Just watching the lads train it was clear how much they wanted it. The focus and attention to detail is all gearing up to winning. I do think after six visits we owe the fans a trophy! For some reason, I don't know what, I have an unshaken faith that we are going to win. If I were a betting man I would lump on us!

It's great to see the lads so happy as a group, it makes dealing with my back a lot easier. I would love to be out there playing and a bit of me is genuinely gutted I can't. I'm sure every player would feel the same, but I understand that the cause of the team is greater and that this set of lads have the ability to win.

28th August

GREAT NEWS this morning that Browny has penned a new contract with the club. He is having a terrific season so far, and with a few games left can accomplish a lot more. A couple of the lads have signed new deals, showing commitment from the club and also from the players to Lancashire, and hopefully this will give them a confidence boost ahead of this weekend.

Jarv and I travelled down this afternoon, braving the M6 on a bank holiday. Lunatics! Arriving what seemed like a day later in Birmingham we ventured out for dinner with the lads. There was an air of calmness about them and you wouldn't have known that they were about to play in the biggest day of the season so far. Having played in a few Finals Days, I've never seen players so relaxed. The air of confidence building around this group is something special, and as long as they can control their emotions tomorrow then I really don't see anyone else winning. We have a strong mix of experience and youth that is perfect for the day.

29th August Finals Day

I WOKE up nervous and I'm not even playing! God knows how the other lads feel. Holly had come down for the day too which was great. We wandered down to breakfast to find a few of the lads were already set up. Pazza had brought his whole family down and there was a really good feeling at breakfast, something I can't really explain, other than that everything just felt right. After breakfast Hol and I took a stroll round Birmingham, more for the benefit of my back than anything else, and fans from all four counties had just started to arrive. It was great to see them all mixing and enjoying the day. Finals Day always has a very friendly atmosphere; it's not like the western terrace at Headingley!

The build up to the semi-final was good as the lads went about their usual routines. Watching the first semi-final between Birmingham and Northants it was clear the pitch didn't have much pace and that cutters and back-of-a-length deliveries would be tough to get away. We discussed this prior to going out and executed perfectly. What a great day for Gavin Griffiths. To make your debut in the semi-final is something special and then to deliver a maiden first over to James Vince-one of the best T20 players in the country-shows just how relaxed he was. It was a great bowling performance all round; the spinners pegged Hampshire back in the middle and the seamers finished off the innings well. To restrict them to 115 was a great effort.

The pitch didn't look the easiest to time the ball on, but Browny made it look pretty straightforward. He was caressing the ball to the boundary and has been in some serious form of late. Browny finished with 45 not out while Jimmy Faulkner put two balls in to the stands to finish the game with an over to go. I didn't go down to the dugout and instead watched from the dressing room balcony, but ended up pacing the balcony about 100 times during game. Watching is certainly harder than playing, but maybe it helped my back!

Advancing to the final was great. Last year we only had a short break of around 30 minutes in-between games due to rain while Birmingham had plenty of time. The dry conditions meant we had a good hour and a half to prepare this time, so we could relax before getting into game mode. As soon as we got through to the final all the talk was about winning and nothing else. Northants are a team full of dangerous players; if one of them comes off they can take the game away from you in a matter of overs. Before the game we had a huddle, and Ash (Ashley Giles) spoke about how nothing else mattered now. This game was everything we had worked towards.

Northants won the toss and chose to bowl, and although we were going to do the same, I do think it played into our hands. The pitch seemed to play a little better. Davo (Alex Davies) played a great knock up top, as did Ashwell, and they got us off to a great start which settled everyone down. Princey played a supporting role at first, while Al scored freely. We looked set for a monster score of around 180-200 at one point, and if we finished up anywhere near there the game would be over.

Then we lost four wickets for seven runs in eight balls, which seriously pegged us back, and completely stopped our momentum. I know momentum gets mentioned a lot in sport, but it is such a massive thing in T20 cricket. The quicker you get it the better, and we had just gone from seeing a possible 180 now becoming 150 which would have only been about par. Arron Lilley, aka The Big Show, then played a little gem of an innings to push us up to 166. If someone had offered me that total in the final at the start of the day I would have snapped their hand off. Scoreboard pressure is massive, and looking at the previous two games it seemed like a pretty big total. The lads said the ball had come on better from the seamers, but crucially it had started to turn.

Defending that sort of total, it's surprising how a few tight overs at the top of the innings can quickly push the asking rate up to ten or more per over before you know it. It makes it a tough ask to score at that rate for 15-16 overs. With two big-hitters in Levi and Willey opening for Northants, containing them was always going to be tough, and sure enough Willey got a few boundaries away while Levi was looking dangerous until Faulks claimed both their wickets. It's at times like these that you want your big name players to step up and on this occasion he did! He's been great for us this season and he certainly turned up today.

After that the wickets kept on falling. Pazza bowling beautifully again; it amazes me how he hasn't been considered for England again since his last inclusion. Things seemed to be going well with Northants needing 86 off the last 8 overs when the wicket of Crook brought 'Boom Boom' Afridi to the crease. I don't think anyone knew what to expect. After trying to hit his first three balls out of Edgbaston and nearly getting out twice in the process, he soon settled and started to strike the ball more and more crisply. My gut instinct though was that he was always going to give a chance. They needed more than ten per over, so big shots were always going to come.

Enter Gavin Griffiths again! Returning to bowl the 18th over with 36 runs needed by Northants you could tell he was clear in his plans and what he wanted to achieve. What everyone didn't know was that he bowled his last nine deliveries with ruptured ligaments in his foot. It's amazing what adrenaline can do! Gav bowled a great over conceding just 7 runs and dismissing Afridi with the third ball-a crucial wicket!

It still wasn't game over at that point as Cobb and Kleinveldt can certainly give it whack, and we needed a great penultimate over. Jimmy Faulkner was just the man. Despite having dislocated a finger a few overs earlier after stopping a blistering Shahid Afridi drive, he showed all his class and experience to bowl a great over leaving Gav to defend 21 off the last.

Surely this was our year now. I must had covered about 20 kilometres walking up and down the balcony by now, probably annoying those sat just below the me, cheering every wicket and certainly losing my voice in the process. It was happening; we were going to win! I couldn't contain my excitement although I had to be careful not to get carried away and forget about my back. Gav looked very calm and bowled a fantastic over.

Northants needed 17 off the last ball and I don't think anyone even noticed it had sailed to third man for 4. We had won! The party started straight away. We had worked so hard just to scrape into the quarter-finals finals and now we were champions for the first time. I couldn't have been prouder of the lads. The elation on their faces showed as we greeted them coming off the field. I confess I had mixed emotions. I was so happy for the boys and the club that we had won the trophy at long last. I just desperately wanted to be out there though. Saying that the club is at the forefront and today was a great day for Lancashire!

Seeing the lads celebrate on the stage moments later certainly spurred me on to playing again and to make sure I got back on the park.

The celebrations were something else! The lads stayed in the changing rooms for a while enjoying the moment, and a few Northants players came in which was great to see after doing battle on the field. I would love to go into more detail about the celebrations, but this is something that was special to the team. Let's just say we had an amazing night!

NatWest T20 Blast
Semi-Final at Edgbaston, 29 August

Hampshire Royals 115 all out (19.5 overs, Vince 69, Parry 3-21, Faulkner 3-29, Lilley 2-11, Edwards 2-16) Lancashire Lightning 119-4 (18.5 overs, Brown 45*)

Lancashire won by 6 wickets

Lancashire faced Hampshire, playing in their sixth consecutive Finals Day, in a repeat of the previous year's semi-final, and once again ran out convincing winners to reach their third T20 Final.

Ashley Giles sprang a surprise before the match, handing a T20 debut to Gavin Griffiths and the 20-year-old responded with a brilliant maiden over to the hard-hitting James Vince, part of England's T20 squad, to start the game superbly. George Edwards, playing in only his sixth T20 game and the first since early June following injury, was just as impressive and the 23-year-old struck first with two wickets in two balls in the sixth over as Hampshire slipped to 33-2.

Owais Shah helped Vince move the total along to 63-2 midway through the ninth over before the Red Rose attack, superbly led by Stephen Parry, turned the game decisively in Lancashire's favour. Parry bowled Shah before trapping both Sean Ervine and Liam Dawson lbw on his way to figures of 3-21. Hampshire now 77-5 at the start of the 13th over failed to wriggle free despite a valiant effort from Vince who was eventually ninth out for 69 off 60 balls as the Lightning bowlers' squeezed the life out of the innings. Arron Lilley finished with a sensational 2-11 from his four overs, including two wickets in two balls to make Hampshire 93-8. Edwards also completed memorable figures of 2-16, while James Faulkner was exceptional at the death claiming two wickets in the final over of the innings to finish with 3-29 as Hampshire collapsed to 115 all out.

Karl Brown then anchored the run chase with a measured 45 not out from 43 balls, which included only four boundaries, to steer Lancashire to a comfortable six-wicket victory. Ashwell Prince and Alex Davies had helped Brown take the score to 52-2 midway through the 8th over and Steven Croft and then Jos Buttler moved that along to 91-4 in the 16th over. Faulkner completed the match with two leg-side sixes off Chris Wood as the win was secured with seven balls to spare.

Lancashire were through to the final where they would face the 2013 winners, Northants Steelbacks following their five-wicket win over the defending champions Birmingham Bears in the first semi-final.

NatWest T20 Blast Final
at Edgbaston, 29 August

Lancashire Lightning 166-7 (20 overs, Davies 47, Prince 43, Afridi 3-14)
Northants Steelbacks 153-6 (20 overs, Cobb 44*, Griffiths 2-23, Faulkner 2-25)

Lancashire won by 13 runs

Unchanged Lancashire, put in to bat by Northants, raced away at the start to get their quest for a first-ever T20 title off to the best possible start. Alex Davies struck a career-best 47 off 26 balls with six fours and a six and Ashwell Prince hit 43 off 45 balls to put 77 runs on the board before Davies was bowled by Josh Cobb off the last ball of the ninth over. Davies had hit a straight six down the ground against left-arm spinner Graeme White in the seventh over, and Jos Buttler repeated the shot in the 13th over to take the score to 103-2. It was the first of two sixes for Buttler, who hit 27 off 15 balls but then became the first of four wickets to fall in eight balls for seven runs as Northants dragged themselves back into the game, with Lancashire now 130-6 two balls into the 16th over. The Red Rose innings was rescued by Arron Lilley with 22 off 17 balls over the closing overs to take Lancashire to 166-7. Would it be enough?

Northants got away to a solid start themselves with 48 runs coming from the first six powerplay overs in reply, but by then James Faulkner had struck two important blows by getting the wickets of Richard Levi, man-of-the-match in the earlier semi-final win over Birmingham, and David Willey. Levi was caught at mid-off by Davies and Willey superbly at mid-wicket by Lilley. The Steelbacks reached halfway at 74-2 with 93 required but Stephen Parry, bowling his third over, had Ben Duckett lbw for 20 with the first ball of the eleventh on the way to figures of 1-23. Steven Croft made that 81-4 in the next over when he had Steven Crook caught at deep mid-wicket.

Cobb and the dangerous Shahid Afridi then put Northants back on course with an exhilarating half-century partnership inside five overs to reach 131-4 after 17 overs with 36 runs required. By then Faulkner was off the field with a dislocated finger, suffered when attempting to stop a blistering Afridi drive in his follow-through two overs earlier, so Griffiths returned to bowl the 18th over and he struck a decisive blow when Afridi struck his third ball to Liam Livingstone at deep cover to depart for 26. Importantly only six runs had been scored from Griffiths' over and a patched-up Faulkner returned to bowl the 19th over that only went for seven more. It left Griffiths, by then nursing a foot injury, to bowl the final over with 21 runs to defend and the youngster capped an utterly memorable day with another wicket, that of Rory Kleinveldt, as he closed out a 13-run victory to clinch Lancashire's first T20 trophy. What a day!

30th August

I WOKE up fully clothed somehow in my hotel room next to Holly. Fair to say she wasn't too impressed! It was a great night (I think!), we didn't venture far from the hotel bar, and I can only say sorry to all the residents who may have heard us singing! Breakfast was interesting, re-living the stories of the day/night. Holly drove us home, and for me it was straight to bed. I was shattered. A day of rest on Sunday was certainly called for.

The lads had travelled in the opposite direction to Kent in preparation for the four-day game. Five points are all we need to secure promotion. If we could manage that, and having won the T20, I would call it a good summer!

31st August

AFTER AN epic weekend it was back to rehab. I swear the pool felt slightly warmer after the success of the weekend, although I was brought crashing back down to reality when asked to perform some basic tasks and couldn't. The enormity of my rehab became pretty clear again. There was some progression as I managed to do some gentle leg exercises which I couldn't before, but that was all. The biggest challenge I have to overcome is trusting my back again. I'm so used to it hurting that the simple task of bending forward fills me with dread. Is it going to hurt? Getting over this challenge won't be easy, and it will be even harder to face the first time I try to play cricket. I keep telling myself to be positive knowing that all will be well, but it will just take time.

SEPTEMBER

Pilates and promotion

Farewell to Ash: making a presentation from the lads to Ashwell Prince after the last home match of the season

1st September

IT FELT a little chillier waking up this morning, maybe it's time to put the heating on! The season seems to have flown by once more, and before we know it we will have begun training for next year! Maybe it's gone quicker for me as I'm so focused on next season now, and the chance to play cricket again gets a bit closer with each day.

Kent seem to be going well at Canterbury. It can be a good batting pitch but if we can sneak a couple of quick wickets we could turn things our way.

2nd September

MY BACK hasn't felt great for the last couple of days; it's been pretty stiff from the new exercises. I worry over every slight twinge, which can be enough to render me useless to anyone. Not knowing what all these new symptoms are is really un-nerving. Rooster is happy with the symptoms I'm feeling and keeps reminding me that recovery isn't a straight line! He wants me to battle through the pain and stiffness to get back to normal.

My biggest problem is I don't know what normal feels like anymore. Learning to trust my back again is key, and without that trust I will struggle to do things properly. Today I thought I had had an 'accident' when in fact it was just the sensation in my legs changing and making them feeling wet! Honestly, I wouldn't wish this on anyone.

3rd September

IT'S BEEN a tough few days for the lads in Kent. Maybe it is a hangover from the T20 win, but whatever the case we are certainly up against it in this fixture. We've seen before this season that when a team gets such a big first-innings score, the mental energy it takes away from you is massive. After fielding for the best part of 150 overs you are pretty cooked. Crofty made a battling 85 with others chipping in around, but unfortunately we couldn't save the follow-on. I feel for Browny who has played well, and for Alviro, both getting out late on. Tomorrow will be a big day, but the prospect of clinching promotion should certainly give the lads an incentive to play well.

My back is easing slowly and "if in doubt do some knee roles" is the line I'm going with at the moment. To be fair they do ease the sensations I'm feeling. I've gone away from my meditation stuff recently so maybe I need to revisit this more often.

4th September

ON A cricket front it's been a great day! Tense I would imagine, if you were watching from the balcony at Kent, but certainly enthralling! Crofty and Alex formed a vital partnership to ensure we avoided defeat and gained promotion. I do think we would have been promoted regardless but the fighting qualities shown by the four batsmen today guaranteed it!

It's a great feeling to know we will be in Division One next season. As a big club that's where we need to be, and I'm sure next year's goal will be to stay up and build a team to move forward. The lads have worked hard all season to achieve this goal; some hard yards have been put in behind closed doors. The little things the public don't see have paid off.

With the T20 in the bag it would be great to do the double. Surrey have gone to the top of the table after their win, making next week's clash between us and them all the more important. It will go a long way to deciding who wins the title!

On the injury front it's not been a pleasant day. My lower back has been really stiff after trying some new exercises. It's to be expected but very unsettling. It's almost like building a new relationship with someone; we are just getting to know each other at the moment. Hopefully we will become best friends!

LV= County Championship Division Two
Game 14 at Canterbury, 1-4 September

Kent 570-8 dec
(Northeast 139, Key 113, Stevens 92, Denly 65)
Lancashire 259 (Croft 85, Brown 53)
& following-on 258-4 (Croft 72*, Davies 58*)

Match Drawn

Rob Key made a measured 113 to frustrating Lancashire at Canterbury as Kent closed on 235-3 on a rain-shortened opening day. Key shared in partnerships of 72 for the first wicket with Daniel Bell-Drummond and 149 for the second wicket with Joe Denly before Jordan Clark struck with two wickets in five balls just before play ended early. Sam Northeast, with a century, and sixth-wicket partner Darren Stevens (92) added to that on the second day with a stand of 183 inside 39 overs either side of lunch as the hosts posted an imposing 570-8 declared.

Lancashire, who started the third day at 25-0, slumped to 101-5 before lunch and were later bowled out for 259. Karl Brown made 53, for his eighth half-century in 13 innings, with Steven Croft's 85 off 170 balls and Jordan Clark's 44 the only other innings of note, the latter pair sharing a sixth-wicket stand of 91 in 25 overs. Unsurprisingly Lancashire, 311 runs behind, were asked to bat again with 16 overs left in the day but, after closing on 47-2, they rallied to finish the match on 258-4 and secure a draw. Croft (72*) and Alex Davies (58*) scored unbeaten fifties and shared an unbroken fifth-wicket partnership of 120, while there were other valuable contributions from Haseeb Hameed with 44 and Ashwell Prince who made 39.

The players shook hands shortly before 5pm, the result finally confirming Lancashire's elevation back to Championship Division One, but meanwhile Surrey had gone top of Division Two with a five-point lead thanks to their win over Derbyshire.

5th September

CONTROVERSY AT the home of cricket! The main talking point I'm sure to come from the one-day international will be the incident involving Ben Stokes when Mitchell Starc threw the ball back down the wicket and hit him on the hand. Did he or didn't he (obstruct the ball)? It's a tough call. As most cricketers have said when a ball like that is thrown at you, your natural reaction is to protect yourself. In my opinion I do feel he was just protecting himself, but what didn't help was that his arm left his 'bubble' if that's the right phrase. It was nowhere near his body making it appear as if he was obstructing the field. It's a debate that will go on for some time, but what it won't change is the result of the game. The Australian one-day machine ploughed through England again, going 2-0 up in the series and looking very comfortable in the process. On the back of a World Cup win they are playing with confidence, whereas England are building for the next one. This England side has a good feel about them. I'm sure after a period of time playing together they will form a solid unit as we saw in the New Zealand series.

My back hasn't felt much better over the last few days; again every little pain is something I read a thousand things into. It's the centre of my universe at the moment and I'm very wary of everything going on. Hopefully it will settle over the weekend.

11th September

BACK IN with the boys at Old Trafford today after they had a few days off following the game against Kent. I think it's been good for them to have a few days apart. During the season you spend every minute of the day with each other so when breaks come in the season, getting away from the group and spending time elsewhere is healthy.

After my Pilates session yesterday the back is a little stiff after it's been put into positions it's not been used to for a while! The exercises put a little stress on the area, and it seems to settle down quickly, but it's also quite unpleasant for a while afterwards. I feel this is something I'm going to have to get used to unfortunately. Every day I wake up thinking how is it going to be today. The symptoms are disappearing slowly, but the fear is always there.

12th September

IT'S NOT often you get to meet your heroes in life. For me today I was lucky enough to spend some time with Sir Ian Botham. Rooster played a blinder sorting it out. Like me, Sir Ian had a bad back injury during his career that kept him on the side-lines for a long spell. To hear him speak about his recovery and what he went through was great. It gave me a great lift moving forward. What struck me most was his mental strength and conviction that he would overcome everything thrown at him. To get this time with such an influential man is very rare, and I'm truly in debt to Rooster.

13th September

THE GREAT weekend continues. Rooster invited me to join his table today for the ODI at Old Trafford. Shame about the result; after the comeback by England it looked set for a great fixture today but it was not to be. It was horrible to see Eoin Morgan get struck on the head. It looked horrific and you could see the distress in Starc's eyes immediately after the event. Hopefully he will be okay.

On the injury front my back seems to be getting better day by day. I feel I can move with much more freedom without having to think about my back. It's an important time as I have to make sure I don't push it too hard. The last thing I need are any setbacks. It's still a patience game and it's certainly testing mine!

15th September

AS THE days keep passing by, I can tell my back is starting to feel a lot stronger. I almost found myself breaking out into a run today and had to stop myself. The thought of Rooster and Sam shouting at me wasn't worth the pain! It's a great sign and shows that I'm moving a lot more naturally now. The confidence this gives me cannot be described. It does however mean I could push myself just a little bit too far, too fast, which certainly isn't worth the risk.

It was a tough day at Old Trafford for the boys. Surrey to their credit played well and ground us down with a mammoth total of 480. I had been looking forward to watching this young lad Sam Curran bowl. He seems to be a bright talent for the future and he certainly showed that with a devastating spell taking three wickets. Finishing the day five down means we will have to play well tomorrow to prevent the follow-on or keep them out there as long as possible. It was sad to see Zafar Ansari leave the field with what seemed to be a bad injury to his bowling hand. He must have been on top of the world this morning having been included in the England touring party. It really was a cruel blow and I hope it's not as bad as it looked.

It was great to see Stephen Parry get a recall into the England T20 squad. He has fully deserved it, bowling consistently well over a number of years now, and everyone at Lancashire is well-chuffed for him.

16th September

ANOTHER TOUGH day at the office for the boys. Again you have to give credit where it is due and Surrey deserve a lot for the way they have played this fixture. Bar a last wicket partnership between Jimmy Anderson and Simon Kerrigan it looked as if we were going to be following-on. With a lead of 208 and a bowler down, Batty decided not to enforce it and give his bowlers some much needed time off. A couple of early blows could have unsettled the away changing room, but the true nature of the pitch came out, although it meant I was lucky enough witness a quite superb century from Kumar Sangakkara. It was a delight to watch his placement of the ball and ability to manipulate the spin was just mind blowing. Surrey eventually declared with seven overs left in the day which, for me was a little bit too late, especially with a lead well over 450. I was pleased to see Browny and Haseeb come through unscathed.

I had my second Pilates session today and what difference a week makes. Last week I felt like a beginner, today I felt stronger and more confident and even able to advance on some of the poses we did last time. Again this is building confidence and each session I have and every movement that I do without any side-effect is massive. Still, I know it's a long road but it's getting shorter every day!

17th September

THE LADS fought hard for the draw today to take the Championship race into the last week of the season. The result today means the double is still alive. A very mature knock of 91 from Haseeb Hameed was the backbone of the innings. He batted for all but three of the overs in the innings and just missed out on what would have a well-deserved hundred. It was the last day of cricket at Old Trafford this season and it's been a great home for us this season, proving to be a fortress in most competitions.

It was also a day that brought to an end to, at least at Old Trafford, the career of Ashwell Prince. The ovation he received leaving the field for the last time was quite something, a true testament to a man that has stood the test of time. We still have one game to go down at Chelmsford but his playing days are now done at Old Trafford. It was quite an emotional evening. I had the honour of presenting him with a gift from the boys and also saying a few words. It was tough to sum up such a great career because he has achieved so much and he played every game for Lancashire as if it was an international game. Hopefully this passion and desire to succeed will remain with us for years to come. I do know it will be certainly missed, as will Ashwell.

LV= County Championship Division Two
Game 15 at Emirates Old Trafford, 14-17 September

Surrey 480 (Ansari 99, Roy 66,
Wilson 51, Burns 50, Kerrigan 4-128)
& 283-7 (Sangakkara 118, Croft 4-35)
Lancashire 272 (S Curran 5-67)
& 195-7 (Hameed 91)

Match Drawn

Lancashire gave a debut to emergency loan signing Phil Mustard, the wicketkeeper standing in for the injured Alex Davies, while James Anderson took his place in the line-up for the first time this season in this clash of the top two teams. It was Surrey who dominated over the first two days after winning the toss, with openers Zafar Ansari and Rory Burns compiling 89 before Burns was bowled by Tom Bailey. Ansari, selected that morning for England's tour to the UAE, fell for 99 to a great catch by Anderson as Surrey closed the day on 262-4. They extended that score with consistent batting on the second day to reach 480 all out, with a 95-run partnership for the 6th wicket between Jason Roy and Gary Wilson the highlight.

Lancashire lost wickets steadily during the evening session to be 141-5 at the close, trailing by 339 runs, and they fared little better on the third day to be all out for 272, with only a last-wicket alliance of 65 runs between Anderson, who made a Lancashire career-best 42, and Simon Kerrigan (23 not out) holding up the Surrey attack, for whom Sam Curran took an impressive 5-67 and his brother Tom 3-54.

Gareth Batty decided against enforcing the follow-on, with spinner Ansari out of action-and sadly out of the England tour-with a broken thumb, and Surrey quickly set about adding to their 208-run lead. Kumar Sangakkara struck a superb 118 which enabled the declaration to arrive at 283-7 giving Lancashire a target of 492. That was always a fairly unrealistic prospect but the Red Rose produced a great rear-guard action on the final day, with 18-year-old Haseeb Hameed, in just his third first-class match, scoring a determined 91. Hameed and Steven Croft batted throughout most of the afternoon to hold up Surrey's quest for the victory with a 91-run partnership in 39 overs. When finally Croft departed for 40 Lancashire were 161-4, but bad light during the final session finally halted play for good with the score on 195-7 with nine overs left.

The draw left Surrey with an eight point advantage going in to the final round of matches.

18th September

AFTER THE emotion of yesterday, today was quite relaxed. I've really upped my walking at the moment. After my chat with Sir Ian Botham I've felt a new surge of encouragement urging me on to get fit. There have been many times when I've felt like throwing in the towel; the monotonous nature of rehab can take its toll. Friday nights are generally saved for some form of entertainment, and tonight mine was the outdoor pool at the gym! It was quite nice actually. I had the pool to myself and, alone with my thoughts, I pictured completing my comeback and playing cricket again.

19th September

LORD'S FINAL time! The domestic 50-over final is always an exciting day in the cricketing calendar. I played in the last one Lancashire reached, and although we lost it was an amazing day. Every cricketer will tell you how good it is, providing you are lucky enough to get there.

It looked like it was going to be Surrey's day, having bowled Gloucestershire out for 220, and I think most were backing them. Having runs on the board, no matter what score, always adds pressure to the side batting second. At 140-2, the trophy looked to be in the bag for Surrey but Gloucester squeezed really well in the middle overs and managed to create chances out of nothing. All of a sudden it was anyone's game and we had a cup final that could have come from a different era. It was proper 'old school' cricket. I was actually quite happy for Gloucester and specifically Geraint Jones who was playing his last ever game. He got vital runs in Gloucester's innings and winning a Lord's final isn't too bad a way to finish I guess!

20th September

IT'S BEEN a relatively relaxing weekend and my back feels great. Throughout this diary I've frequently mentioned the importance of rest. I've had it drummed into me! If you don't let your body adapt to what you're putting it through, you will never improve. A nice early walk and some Pilates exercises was all that was needed today. Making sure I'm fresh for the week's training is just as important!

21st September

A TYPICAL rainy day in Manchester. The boys are preparing for what will be the final game of the season, and it's a very important one. We might be promoted now, but we want to be champions. Winning silverware is always good for the spirit of everyone connected with the club and those who support us.

For me it was another day of rehab. Walking, swimming and walking again. The routine is simple, the monotony mind-numbing, but the end goal outweighs everything. I'm making good progress, my back feels strong and the strength in my foot is starting to return.

22nd September

THERE IS still a lot to play for in both divisions of the Championship with the battle for relegation in the First Division and who will be crowned Division Two champions still to be decided. For us it was a soggy wet day in Essex with no play taking place which was very frustrating. It reminded me of the last game of 2011; we could only concentrate on our game and nowhere else. The same applies this week. We can't control what Surrey do, we just need to focus on what we do. It's great to see the two leagues coming down to the last game, and it goes to show that every point you get in April and May is just as important and crucial and should never be overlooked.

For me I must admit I'm ready for the season to end. The lads have achieved so much and I could not be more chuffed for them. They have played with a passion and a commitment to Lancashire that has been great to see. I'm ready for the end now so I can focus on getting fit and making next year even better.

I'm excited about the winter plans that lie ahead, I'm still a little unsure as to what I want to do but I certainly feel a lot more comfortable in myself coming towards the back end of my career.

Fingers crossed all goes well with my rehab and I'll be back out there.

23rd September

PILATES TODAY with Kim. She was impressed with my progression from last week and we were able to advance my movements a bit further, pushing my back a little more than last week. There has been no reaction as yet from anything I've done. This might sound funny, but if I ever get a strange sensation I always check my toes. They were the first to lose the sensation of feeling before the operation, so I know that if I can feel them I'm generally okay!

The weather was a little better down in Essex with a full day being managed. It looked promising after winning the toss and having Essex in trouble on 29-3, and it took a fantastic counter-attack from Ravi Bopara and Jesse Ryder to turn things around. Ryder made a rapid century at nearly a run a ball and Bopara a more gritty 99. The Chelmsford pitch can certainly flatten out with the sun on it, and the margin for error can be slight. Jimmy got us back in the game with a couple of late strikes with the second new ball and although they finishing the day on 328-7, if we can knock them over tomorrow morning and go big, a win is still on the cards. Surrey have had a good day though, Kumar Sangakkara signing off with a century. The title is still on but we will have to play well.

24th September

TODAY WAS about everything away from cricket. Holly had her 12 week scan and understandably was quite nervous. All was well though and her mind was set at ease about a number of things. Next season will be a bit different with a little one to contend with!

The lads looked to be fighting back at Essex with Jimmy showing all his class in taking 7-77 from 31 overs, and young Haseeb again showing why everyone is tipping him for big things with a well-made 63. At 131-2 the game is in the balance, on what seems a good pitch. Some 'negotiating' may need to be done to create some sort of result, but time will tell.

I'm sure Ashwell will want to go out with a bang on his last day of cricket tomorrow. It will be a strange feeling for him I'm sure, but he can safely say he has had a career he can be very proud about.

25th September

BY ALL accounts the season finished on an exceptionally dull day down at Chelmsford. It's always a sad occasion when the last day comes along, and more so this morning for Ashwell Prince. He spent nearly six seasons at Lancashire and after averaging very close to 50 and with 15 hundreds, it's fair to say he's had a good crack. I followed the game on the radio this morning and from the descriptive nature of the stroke play it sounded like Ash was determined to go out with a bang. Having reached his fifty, he was out straight away, but I'm sure everyone on the ground was hoping for a special hundred to see him off in style. He has been a great servant to the club and inspired many of the next generation of players to move forward in their careers.

That moment sparked a slight collapse with the last seven wickets falling for 100 runs, but so much play has been lost to the weather this week only an 'arranged' game could have manufactured a result. It wasn't the case and the game petered out into a draw. It was quite an anti-climax to what could have been a very entertaining week of cricket. We can't help the weather! Surrey ended up being Division Two champions and they have played some good cricket and fully deserved their title. For us it was a job done to gain promotion back to Division One.

I'm sure the lads will all go away and reflect on the season from a personal view and a team perspective. There have been lot of positives to take from the season with several younger players coming through and getting a taste of first team cricket.

We can't forget the T20 win. What a day-and night! It has been a goal of ours over the last few years to win a one-day competition and we have come so close on a number of occasions. Getting over the line this year will hopefully breed future success.

We have a very talented squad here at Lancashire, and as always we are backed up by our fans who follow us through thick and thin. The support I have had this year has been amazing. In some dark days the support of you, the fans, and my team-mates has pulled me through. I can't wait to get cracking again next season.

LV= County Championship Division Two Game 16 at Chelmsford, 22-25 September

Essex 394 (Ryder 116, Bopara 99, Anderson 7-77) & 138-3 (Bopara 52*) Lancashire 310 (Reece 82, Hameed 63, Prince 51)

Match Drawn

Looking to better Surrey's result if they were to grab the second division title, the last thing Lancashire needed was any rain delays, but that is precisely what they got as the first day at Chelmsford was washed away. When play did get under way on day two, Glen Chapple struck twice and Jimmy Anderson once as the hosts slipped to 29-3 inside 12 overs but the Red Rose attack was then frustrated by a rapid 138-ball century from Jesse Ryder and 99 by Ravi Bopara, the pair adding 186 inside 51 overs for the fourth wicket. A fifty by Ryan tenDoeschate helped Essex to a total of 394 on the third day, Anderson finishing with a Lancashire-best 7-77.

Teenage opener Haseeb Hameed then underpinned a Red Rose response of 131-2 by the close with a measured 63, while Luis Reece-who top-scored with 82-and retiring star Ashwell Prince both scored half-centuries in an 81-run partnership on the fourth day as the game drifted to a draw. In the final innings of his career, Prince scored 51 off 38 balls and seemed intent on going out playing his shots. After receiving a guard of honour from the Essex players upon his arrival at the crease, the South African scored 37 runs from his first 26 balls, hitting seven fours in a nine-ball spell, including five successive fours against Ryder's medium pacers.

Lancashire slipped from 281-4 to 310 all out and although Essex were quickly 10-2, Bopara and Tom Westley steadied matters with a 70-run partnership as the draw was agreed at 4.20pm with Essex 138-3.

Surry's draw with Northants ensured the Division Two title went to the Oval, with Lancashire ending as runners-up but delighted to be returning to the top flight in 2016.

POSTSCRIPT

On the road to recovery

*Back in the nets: chatting to Academy Director
Gary Yates in the Cricket Centre*

29th February, 2016

IT'S THE end of February, the new season is only fifty days away, and a lot has happened in the five months since my final diary entry in September.

I've made the transition from recovering as a patient to rehabilitating as a cricketer, an important step!

The first thing I did once the season ended was go abroad to attend Karl and Jenny Brown's wedding in Marbella. That was a great occasion, while it was also good for me to get away from the cricketing side of things for a few days.

Then it was back to my rehab. The players came back to start training in November and I slowly started getting into batting again. Just a few little underarm feeds from Sam, but it felt great to be holding a bat once more. I was also allowed to do a very short jog in the Indoor Centre nets, 20-odd yards or so, but I felt a real sense of achievement as if just I'd climbed Everest!

I had to reign myself in after that because the temptation is always there for you to do more. I had to be really diligent with my rehab, and got great help from Sam and Rooster who were ever-present and really good with me.

Batting properly again started when we returned for nets in the New Year. It went really well too - I was thrilled. It was funny though; Tom Bailey was lined up to bowl at me and he asked Sam, who was behind the net, 'what do you want me to do? 'Don't bowl anything short!' Sam hollered back up the wicket anxiously. He was right though - having to hook the first ball probably wouldn't have been the wisest thing to do!

In fact, I had to go through a routine of practising every different type of shot I normally play. It meant I had keep playing each shot over and over again, until I got back into the groove of playing it naturally. It was repetitive, but necessary, and after all the rehab it was also good fun.

Since then I've progressed to facing the bowlers day in day out and I'm playing now as a normal batter would do, including dealing with the short stuff. I'm not getting any special treatment!

Just like the batting, I've had to build things up slowly with the bowling. Start off with a few drills and steadily build it up to where I'm running in properly. The first time I must admit was a bit nerve-wracking. As you run in you think 'is it going to hurt' and almost expect it hurt. But it didn't and that's such a great feeling. Each little improvement you do is like getting over another hurdle.

This week I've taken another big step; back-to-back bowling sessions for the first time, and it's gone well. I'm also running in off my full run-up and got my first wicket again the other day! Not sure Arron Lilley was too impressed though!

Fielding-wise I've progressed to diving routines now, using the crash mats. I started with the bigger mats and have moved on to the softer ones that are more realistic to what it feels like diving out on the field. I'm still doing my Pilates with Kim, and I have a daily routine of core work to keep to as well. There's the daily swim and I enjoy that because I know it's helping me to return to cricket. I go quite early when it's quiet because it's both relaxing and good to have a bit of time to myself.

Every day I wake up now, the first thing in my mind is 'how will it feel today'? You just have to deal with that and get on with it. I go back to the chats I had with the likes of Sir Ian Botham who overcame a possible career-ending injury to play for England and that gives you a great deal of encouragement.

I'm very lucky to be back playing cricket, and pleased things are going well. I didn't really expect to be so far down the line by the end of February and a lot of credit must go to the medical staff for that.

I'm under no illusion though. I'm a recovering cricketer but just recovering itself won't be enough to get me back in the team. I've got to be playing good cricket to do that.

I've no set targets, although if I can be available for selection for the first game that would be awesome. If not, it's not a big issue. I'm going away on the pre-season tour to the UAE, which is great because it's come at the ideal time, but I'm trying not to get too far ahead of myself. But moving from indoor work to outdoors will be perfect.

This last week I've joined in with all the squad fitness sessions, and for me that's was great. It shows I'm not that far away from the fitness levels of the rest of the team. I found that really encouraging, but at the same time, having learned what's right for my body, I know now not to get too carried away with what the lads are doing. They're all fully fit and doing what they need to do for their own preparations.

I've also been busy taking coaching courses. I found that I learned a lot from sitting on the side-lines last year just watching games. You see how your lads play as well as the opposition, and you learn from seeing how different tactics are being used. You are always learning at this game! I'm doing my level 3 coaching course at the moment and would like to go on to do level 4 – providing I pass! I've got to look to the future and if I can stay in the game after my playing days that would be great.

One of the biggest learning curves I've had from this time on the side-lines is that cricket is just one part, albeit an important one, of my life. Holly and me are about to have a baby (in April) and that gives you a new focus and a different outlook.

I can't believe now how quickly the start of the new season has come around. My philosophy is to take everything day by day now and don't take anything for granted. I work hard every day to make sure my back is alright and do all the boring things involved in that process well. If that means getting up at 6.30am to go the gym, then that's what I have to do.

I can't wait to get out on the field and play for Lancashire again. I've got a special celebration planned for when I get my first wicket! I hope you are there to see it.

Smudger
February 2016

SHERLOCK HOLMES
& THE BIRTH OF THE ASHES

By Arunabha Sengupta

The Oval, 1882. WG Grace, the great champion of England cricket, and Fred 'The Demon' Spofforth, that diabolical Australian bowler, are locked in a titanic tussle as England and Australia play out a thriller of a match. That was the day when giants clashed, sparks flew and it resulted in the lore of The Ashes. We know all about that.

But, it has seldom been revealed that in the pavilion on that famous August day sat Sherlock Holmes, his services recruited by Charles W Alcock, Secretary of the Surrey County Cricket Club. After a century and a third thereof, the facts of the matter have finally been made public; Dr John Watson's account of the sensational events have at long last seen the light of the day.

We are taken on a journey of knuckle-cracking, nail-biting cricket action along with suspense, tension, villainy and death, and the Birth of the Ashes.

A gourmet treat for the lovers of Sherlock Holmes, mystery stories, as well as a delight for the cricket fans.

Price £6 post free from:

Max Books. Epworth House 34 Wellington Road, Nantwich, Cheshire CW5 7BX.

A publisher specialising in Books on Lancashire Cricket and Crime/Detection stories.
Also Limited edition books on Lancashire Cricket.
Please apply for more details.

www.max-books.co.uk